# Fired by the Canadian Government for Criticizing Islam

# *Fired*

## by the Canadian Government for Criticizing Islam

*Multicultural Canada: A Weak Link in the Battle Against Islamization*

By Christine Douglass-Williams

September 2018

Center for Security Policy Press

For more information about this book, visit
SECUREFREEDOM.ORG

*Fired by the Canadian Government for Criticizing Islam*
is published in the United States
by the Center for Security Policy Press,
a division of the Center for Security Policy.

ISBN-13: 978-1727738438
ISBN-10: 1727738438

The Center for Security Policy
Washington, D.C.
Phone: 202-835-9077
Email: info@SecureFreedom.org
For more information, visit SecureFreedom.org

Book design by Bravura Books

# TABLE OF CONTENTS

# FOREWORD

Those who would stifle free speech are drawing ever closer to home. After all, the forces of tyranny—whether communist, fascist, globalist, or Islamic—know that unfettered free speech is the front line of defense against subjugation of the individual to the domination of the collective. Constraining free speech is thus always the first step to crushing the human right to freedom of belief and conscience.

Canadian Christine Douglass-Williams, who writes for the online publication *Jihad Watch*, a project of the David Horowitz Freedom Center directed by Robert Spencer, knows this full well and, unfortunately, firsthand. Ms. Douglass-Williams, an immigrant to Canada from the Caribbean nation of Trinidad and Tobago, served as an appointed Director on the Board of Directors for the Canadian Race Relations Foundation (CRRF) from 2012-2017, until she was summarily removed on the basis of specious accusations of "Islamophobia."

As a member of a racial minority in Canada herself, Ms. Douglass-Williams is dedicated to principles of individual liberty, equality for all before the law and defense of the rights of minority populations. So, she wrote—on her own time—at *Jihad Watch* to warn her adopted country, and the West in general, of a rising tide of Sharia-supremacism that aims, among other things, to ban and punish harshly the exercise of just such human rights. The Queen's Privy Council on the advice of Canada's then-Heritage Minister Melanie Joly, retaliated by terminated her appointment as a Governor in Council Appointee on December 20, 2017.

The Center for Security Policy has long been concerned about the seemingly inexorable, if incremental, slide of our northern neighbor towards authoritarianism. This is especially evident with regard to official restrictions on expression critical of the rising influence of the Muslim Brotherhood and the broader global Islamic Movement.

Christine Douglass-Williams' experiences exemplify the ominous impact of such behavior on the part of the Canadian government and quasi-official Human Rights Commissions on Canadians' ability to enjoy the intrinsic human rights guaranteed to them in the Canadian Charter of Rights and Freedoms. Hence, the Center invited Ms. Douglass-Williams to document her experiences.

This monograph, *Fired by the Canadian Government for Criticizing Islam—Multicultural Canada: A Weak Link for Islamization*, is her deeply personal account of what was done to her. But it is also something much more important. For, while the arbitrary and discriminatory treatment of an individual Canadian citizen is a story worth telling in its own right, its broader implications for the future of free expression and all other individual rights in that important Western nation that makes this work so valuable.

It is no small irony that—even though Christine Douglass-Williams has long been *and remains* committed to the idea that her country is a diverse and multicultural one and that such qualities are to be prized within the framework of loyalty and patriotism to Canada—in the end, it was for her ostensible "intolerance" that she was fired.

Ms. Douglass-Williams deeply appreciates and champions the universal freedoms heralded in her country's national anthem, "O Canada." She is also keenly aware of both the history of racial discrimination in the Americas and the reality that it was Judeo-Christian-based Western Civilization that abolished slavery—even as it remains lawful under Sharia to this day. But, because she pointed out that Sharia principles are, in fact, liberty-crushing and have no place in a free society like Canada's, the government of Prime Minister Justin Trudeau took the side of both Leftists and Sharia-supremacists who seek to obliterate independent thought and impose that totalitarian code's prohibitions against "blasphemy" and "slander" on its once-free citizens. Stigmatizing her reporting for *Jihad Watch* as "bigotry" and "racism," the Canadian government did, in fact, the bidding of the forces of tyranny.

Christine Douglass-Williams had a further exposure to this phenomenon as a member of a multinational delegation of civil society groups, including the Center for Security Policy, that attended a recent meeting of the Organization for Security and Cooperation in Europe (OSCE). The organization's Office of Democratic Institutions and Human Rights (ODIHR) convened its annual Human Dimensions Implementation Meeting (HDIM) in September 2018 in Warsaw. Her participation there afforded Ms. Douglass-Williams an opportunity to witness personally the gathering chorus of hard-core cultural Marxists in witting collaboration with the Organization of Islamic Cooperation (OIC) that is demanding imposition of "hate speech" and "hate crime" legislation. The shocking reality is that this is no longer occurring only in places subjugated to Sharia, but in the West, as well. She joined colleagues from the United States, Austria, Britain, Denmark, France, Poland, and elsewhere in delivering impassioned speeches to the conference's plenary sessions with a common theme of denouncing and rejecting any such restraints on the right of free people to speak their minds and beliefs.

And yet, the sorts of warnings that Ms. Douglass-Williams and others eloquently expressed in Poland have gone unheeded in her own country. Instead, with support from the governing Liberal Party, one of its Muslim Members of Parliament, Iqra Khalid, successfully proposed a motion (M-103) in the House of Commons demanding that "Islamophobia" be treated as a crime—absent even any definition of the supposed offense. As Douglass-Williams explains in these pages:

> *Motion M103 calls on the government to "condemn Islamophobia and all forms of systemic racism and religious discrimination," asks the government to "recognize the need to quell the increasing public climate of hate and fear," and requests for the "Commons Heritage Committee to study how the government could develop a government-wide approach to reducing or eliminating systemic racism and religious discrimination, including Islamophobia, and collect data to provide context for hate crime reports and to conduct needs assessments for impacted communities."*

Behind this drive to strip Canadians of the right to free speech about Islam's totalitarian Sharia doctrine are groups like the National Council of Canadian Muslims (NCCM), which formerly did business as the Council on American-Islamic Relations Canada (CAIR-CAN). CAIR is a front for Hamas, the Palestinian-Gaza branch of the Muslim Brotherhood and a designated foreign terrorist organization by the U.S. government. Additionally, CAIR was named by the Department of Justice as an unindicted co-conspirator in the 2008 Holy Land Foundation terrorism funding trial. Khalid was a former president of the York University chapter of another Muslim Brotherhood front group, the Muslim Student Association (MSA).

The adoption of M-103 and the firing of Christine Douglass-Williams are manifestations of the steady alignment of the Canada's government and elites with their counterparts in the Western European hard left, as well as the international forces of the Islamic Movement led by the OIC and Muslim Brotherhood. While most Canadians and Americans alike will agree that racism and intolerance based only on bias and hatred are inimical to our founding principles, "Islamophobia" remains undefined—not just in Canadian law, but anywhere.

The practical effect of vilifying such a made-up condition, though, is to insinuate Sharia's prohibitions on any criticism of Islam, which its adherents call "blasphemy" or "slander"—actions that *are* strictly defined under in the Sharia code and can carry the death penalty. Thus, elements of the Brotherhood in Canada that are working assiduously to insinuate such anti-free-speech elements into Canadian law are advancing the agenda of the Organization of Islamic Cooperation which is working to impose Sharia's anti-blasphemy rules worldwide.

We who enjoy the privilege of living in still-free societies that guarantee equality under the rule of man-made law must stand together in opposing the Sharia-supremacists' efforts to impose their totalitarian program on us. This book offers a most helpful and timely insight into just how close to home such efforts now are—and a warning of the degree to which similar lines of attack are being advanced by the civilization jihadists in our own country, as well.

Frank J. Gaffney, Jr.
President and CEO
Center for Security Policy

# INTRODUCTION

I, Christine Douglass-Williams, was terminated as Director on the Board of Directors for the Canadian Race Relations Foundation (CRRF) by the Queen's Privy Council on the advice of Canada's Heritage Minister Melanie Joly, four months after receiving a threatening letter from Joly about my writings on political Islam for the online publication Jihad Watch, directed by Robert Spencer and a project of the David Horowitz Freedom Center in California. Melanie Joly was moved to a Tourism portfolio in July 2018 during a Cabinet shuffle, but I reference her position in the present form as key events unfolded that relate to her influence as Heritage Minister.

The CRRF is an 'arms-length' Federal Government agency—and Crown Corporation—which was established as an outcome of the signing of the Japanese Redress Agreement of 1988 between Prime Minister Brian Mulroney and redress leader Art Miki. Ironically, 'arms-length' means *independent of* under contract law, despite having mutual interests.

I was appointed to the CRRF in 2012 under the Conservative Stephen Harper government, and reappointed in 2015. At that time, the CRRF functioned under the Department of Citizenship and Immigration and Minister Jason Kenny. After the election of the Liberal Government, the foundation was placed under the Department of Heritage, of which Melanie Joly became Minister. It is also worthwhile to note that I became an External Adviser to the Office of Religious Freedom in June 2015; that office was shut down immediately after Justin Trudeau became Prime Minister of Canada. The office, which denounced draconian blasphemy laws globally, was originally dedicated to Shahbaz Bhatti, a Christian who was minister of minorities in Pakistan who openly opposed Pakistan's blasphemy laws and was assassinated for doing so by Pakistani jihadis.

Joly made good on her written threat to have me removed as a Director with the CRRF under fabricated accusations of 'Islamophobia.' The Privy Council terminated my appointment as a Governor in Council Appointee on December 20, 2017, despite my years of dedicated commitment to the Foundation, on which I also served as Chair of the Investment Committee, a member of the Human Resource, Executive and former Nominations Committees. I also served as a jurist in assessing the best practices of organizations and individuals in promoting harmonious race relations from nationwide submissions for the CRRF biennial Award of Excellence Gala.

The reason for my CRRF termination was for criticizing political Islam on Jihad Watch, on my own time, and because of *My Personal Warning to Icelanders*, which was published on Jihad Watch and translated for publication in Iceland's largest newspaper, the *Morgunbladid*. In the article, I warned about the deceptions that Muslim Brotherhood and Islamic supremacist operatives used in their goals of subversion in the West. Their tactics are well-documented.

I personally make a distinction between those Muslims who choose to practice Islam in peace and with respect for the separation from mosque and state, and those more devout Muslims dedicated to the shariah imperative to jihad with their agenda to usurp democratic constitutions, demand special privileges over other creeds, and attack non-Muslims as an obligation of the faith. I make this distinction clear in my book, *The Challenge of Modernizing Islam* (Encounter Books, 2017). It is odd to be removed from a race relations foundation for my private work in criticizing the range of abuses that are characteristic of authoritative Islamic doctrine, particularly in light of the fact that Islam is not a race. In the following pages, the reason will become more apparent as I tell my story, which illustrates a disturbing picture of how I was made a public example as Canada marches to the orders of Muslim Brotherhood operatives.

# PART 1



## MY CRRF ADVOCACY AND VISION FOR UNITY

As I prepared to document the events leading up to my termination of duties at the CRRF, I sorted through the hundreds of emails reflecting the trying times and earlier fine ones as our Executive team and board strove for a united Canada.

During my years with the CRRF, I contributed to ideas of youth engagement, Canada-wide lectures and round tables, because I believed that all Canadians should participate in the evolution of Canada's democracy under a banner of multiculturalism, under which immigrants were inevitably bringing in their myriad cultural practices and imported conflicts. I was of the conviction that responsible leadership was fundamental in maintaining Canadian democratic rights and freedoms for all, regardless of color, creed, and culture.

I understood the truth about racism and intolerance between visible minority groups. For example, Afghans are treated deplorably in Iran, and racism and colorism are found in abundance in the country of my birth, Trinidad. One difficulty I had with certain CRRF stakeholders was their indignant approach toward white people, European culture, and history. The messages conveyed at the CRRF Award of Excellence gala, programs, and roundtables were sometimes disturbing to me, as many guest speakers condemned only one kind of racism and bigotry from the podium: that of white people against black people; white people against natives; white people against Muslims.

The board knew my sentiments, but the challenge in organizations is to keep stakeholders satisfied. In the view of the standardized victimology stakeholders, the evolution of modern-day multicultural Canada, free of systemic, state-driven interracial conflict and full of opportunities for visible minorities, did not matter.

It also was not discussed that many community leaders perpetuated their own disadvantage and oppression through hatred of white people and conflict within their own family structures and communities, which was also deemed to be the white people's fault. All the while, other countries still held black slaves and practiced misogyny and the worst kind of abuses against fellow human beings. Topping the list of such abusers were Islamic supremacists, who also sought to obliterate the nation of Israel out of bigotry against Jews and which propagated a code of laws [shariah] that assigned special status based on gender, race and religion. One lady from the black community once drew my attention when she publicly declared onstage during a CRRF symposium that blacks and Jews suffer the worst hate crimes, so why was it that all everyone heard about was 'Islamophobia'?

**Our Canada**

As I continued to sort through emails, I was reminded of a casual off-CRRF premises meeting between members of the Executive CRRF team and external contributors to brainstorm on possible ideas for youth engagement in multicultural Canada. I retained the email of my own contribution toward fostering Canadian values and harmony. As a patriotic Canadian, I was inspired to suggest an idea for implementation as part of a program for youth. This was my submitted documentation, which I sent via an email on the morning of August 26, 2014:

> *The whole project can possibly be centered around the Theme "Oh Canada" and even named "Our Canada" related to our national anthem. What the concept of "Our Canada" means can be a question asked and a concept built upon and outlined for students.*

**Perhaps we can use the national anthem to illustrate points:**

O Canada!
Our home and native land!
True patriot love in all thy sons command.
*Considerations: how does each and every Canadian make this their home and their Canada while being loyally patriotic and loving toward country?*
With glowing hearts we see thee rise,
The True North strong and free!
*Considerations: what are ways to build a strong Canada in unity and keep it free and strong?*
From far and wide,
O Canada, we stand on guard for thee.
*Considerations: what does this statement mean? It suggests that everyone far and wide has a responsibility toward Canada.*
God keep our land glorious and free!
O Canada, we stand on guard for thee.

O Canada, we stand on guard for thee.

*Consideration: a final solidification of the whole meaning of "Our
Canada," with the evolved theme of: This is Our Canada so let's build it
together and let's protect it together.*

**Building on Operation Thank you can be a sub-category
under "Our Canada" called "Operation Welcome"** signifying that
to enable our national anthem—to help us stand on guard
together—we need to welcome one another so what are ways that
every single group in the country can work on welcoming the other
especially those who hate one another from "back home" and how
can all Canadians work together and facilitate that?

**A section on Canadian Human Rights and our Constitution
and laws** can also be presented as documents to protect all
Canadians and all Canadians (in order to stand on guard) need to do
their part to preserve the meaning of those documents for the good
of Canada.  In this scenario, lots of art and caricatures can be used to
"soften" a hard message.

# Registered Letter from Canadian Heritage Minister M.P. Melanie Joly

There was a series of events leading up to the receipt of a registered letter of warning from Canada's Heritage Minister, Melanie Joly.

**May 22, 2017**

CRRF Chairman Albert Lo called me personally at home to inquire about a reporter from Iceland who had been emailing and calling the Foundation repeatedly for days, as well as the Heritage Department, accusing me of being anti-Muslim, stemming from my talk in Iceland and my Útvarp Saga radio station warning about hate speech in mosques and my open view in defense of mosque surveillance. This reporter—confirmed to be Bjartmar O.Þ. Alexandersson—demanded answers as to why I would be serving in a federal anti-racism organization, to which he was given "no comment."

**June 6, 2017**

Mr. Lo, with a markedly tense tone to his voice, phoned me again to subtly deliver the message that I was being watched by certain bureaucrats in the Department of Heritage. I told him that "whoever put you up to this, please tell him or her to put their concerns in writing."

**July 18, 2017**

I received an early afternoon phone call from the office of Graham Flack, Deputy Minister of Heritage, with a follow-up email "Invitation from Graham Flack" for a teleconference with him, which read: "Graham Flack & Christine Douglass-Williams. We will call Ms. Williams at...(home #)...Friday, Jul 21, 2017 from 11 AM to 11:20 AM."

I mulled over this request, recalled Mr. Lo's tense phone call, and made the decision minutes later to cancel the meeting, requesting to "please send any conversation you would like to have in writing either in an email or by mail."

**July 25, 2017**

A registered letter arrived at my home from the Minister of Heritage Melanie Joly:

You are in trouble. Your numbers are too small in a vast land to continue as you are, in allowing Islamic supremacist incursion into your country as you have. You have unwittingly allowed it, being taken in by your own acceptance and tolerance of immigrants, which is admirable. Your nation has evolved, as all Western states have evolved, to be willing to welcome minorities from every country of the globe, and you have implemented a constitution that declares the equality of everyone under the law. But you need street smarts with regard to immigrants. Islamic supremacists will smile at you, invite you to their gatherings, make you feel loved and welcome, but they do it to deceive you and to overtake you, your land and your freedoms. They intentionally make you feel guilty for questioning their torturous deeds toward humanity— toward women, Christians, gays, Jews, apostates, infidels and anyone who dares to oppose these deeds. If they were genuine, they would make no apologies for such abuses globally, but they would offer to make amends by contributing to the reform of the thinking of their coreligionists, bringing them to deem all humans to be equal in their eyes. They would not accuse you of racism if you question them, which you should do if you really care about the lives and well-being of your fellow human beings globally.

2. "Canada moving toward criminalizing "Islamophobia," January 28, 2017:

A big question to bear in mind is why the "Islamophobia" motion was "unanimously" agreed upon in Parliament. What happened to the few Conservative members present? And to the interim leader of the Conservative Party of Canada, and official opposition, Rona Ambrose? Were they, too, intimidated into submission at the expense of Canadians?

This incursion of Islamic supremacists and their allies and lapdogs peddling their wares into Canadian Parliament is a grave concern.

3. "I was challenged:  Why Write About Jihadists and Muslim Migrant Crimes?," June 10, 2016:

How many Westerners want our cities and countries to become replicas of Islamic states, with the full range of all the atrocities committed in them? We're on our way there, folks, unless we hold leaders accountable; those who should be protecting the citizens of our countries from bloodthirsty criminals and people who are encroaching upon our freedoms and safety.

Some of these people cannot fathom modern-day truth about the bloodthirsty hatred and evil zeal of Jihadists, who ultimately aim to destroy our freedoms in the name of a religion that is historically rooted in war and conquest; and most importantly, is still carrying out that war today, both militarily and insidiously. And since 1948, Muslims have killed over 10 million of their co-religionists, as well as thousands of non-Muslims.

In light of the foregoing, I am concerned with your continued role as a director on the Board of Directors and I am considering whether to recommend to the GIC that your appointment be terminated. However, before I make my decision I am prepared to hear from you.

As your appointment is during the pleasure of the Government, it may be terminated at any time, with or without cause. I ask that by close of business on August 11, 2017, you provide me with any representations, in writing, that you believe should be taken into account before a decision is made regarding your continued appointment as a director of the CRRF. Before I decide whether or not to make any recommendation to the GIC, I will carefully consider your written submissions. Should I proceed with a recommendation, the GIC will consider your representations along with my submission and will ultimately determine whether or not to terminate your appointment. Any termination would be effected through the use of an Order in Council. If you would like more information on this process, I would encourage you to speak to Janine Sherman, Deputy Secretary to the Cabinet (Senior Personnel and Public Service Renewal) at 613-957-5465.

Sincerely,

The Honourable Melanie Joly, P.C., M.P.
Minister of Canadian Heritage

## August 14, 2017

An email arrived to fellow board member Kandy, who gave me permission to use her name, but I chose not to use her full name for her own protection:

*From: Nicole Brockbank*
*Sent: Monday, August 14, 2017 1:02 PM*
*To: Kandy xxxx*
*Subject: Canadian Race Relations Foundation question*

*Hi Kandy,*

*I'm a journalist with CBC News Toronto. I couldn't find any contact information (phone or email) for the board of directors of the Canadian*

*Race Relations Foundation on the website, so I thought I'd reach out here.*

*I'm just wondering if I could have a quick chat with you by phone? I've received some information in a tip that I'd like to talk with you about off the record.*

*You can reach me at my desk at xxxx*

**August 15, 2017**

An email was sent out by a member of the Executive Committee to all board members and newly appointed members, whom I had not met:

*I am writing you as xxxx and on behalf of Albert Lo, Chairperson of the CRRF. Albert is travelling in the United States and does not have easy access to a computer.*

*At least three members of the Board have received calls and notes from a CBC reporter based on "a tip from one of our viewers." It was further claimed that the reporter could not find numbers or e-mails of whom to contact at CRRF and was "just looking for an off the record comment."*

*I want to thank the Board members who have already referred the calls to xxxx but would like to state our protocol for all members at the same time.*

*Only xxxx are spokespersons for the CRRF. All media calls either on or off the record should be referred to xxxx whose e-mail address is included in the addresses above. She will decide on the best course of action, to refer the call to xxxxx or to deal with it herself. On matters relating to CRRF it is essential that we speak with one voice.*

*We will have the chance to go over the details and rationales of the external communications policy at the upcoming orientation and Board meeting in October.*

*Until then, thank you for your cooperation and support on this very important matter.*

**August 18, 2017**

In an email to me:

*Hi Ms. Douglass-Williams,*

*My name is Stephanie Levitz and I'm a reporter with The Canadian Press.*

*I'm writing in connection to your role as a board member of the Canadian Race Relations Foundation. It's come to my attention that concerns have been raised within the foundation, and also within government, about your writings on Jihad Watch and whether they are compatible with your work on the board. I've been further informed that those concerns have resulted in a process being initiated to review your position.*

*I'd like to hear your side of the story and wonder if you had some time to speak today. I can be reached via this email or by phone at xxxx. I do intend to publish a story about the issue.*

*Stephanie*

Two days later, the story broke into mainstream media: *"Federal appointee to race relations board under scrutiny for writings on Islam."*

I was subsequently heartened by the many letters in my defense that were sent to Melanie Joly, along with a few to Chairman Albert Lo. A petition was started by lawyer Robert Onley, son of former Lieutenant Governor of Ontario David Onley to *"Keep Christine Williams on Canadian Race Relations Foundation Board & Protect Free Speech."*[2] It drew 1,323 signatures before becoming obsolete due to my firing. The petition was also promoted by well-known University of Toronto Psychologist Jordan B. Peterson who tweeted out: "Keep Christine Williams on the Canadian Race Relations Foundation Board."

Robert Spencer wrote Melanie Joly his personal letter:

Honorable Minister Joly:

I am writing in support of Christine Douglass-Williams, a member of the Canadian Race Relations Foundation, who I understand has come under scrutiny for writing for my web publication, Jihad Watch.

The Canadian Press has identified as questionable one specific piece that Ms. Douglass-Williams published at Jihad Watch (among other places), in which she refers to deceptive Islamic supremacists. However, neither the Canadian

Press nor anyone else has offered any evidence for why what Ms. Douglass-Williams wrote was wrong or hateful.

In the piece, she referred to Muslims who posture as moderate when they actually aren't. Do such people actually exist? Consider the imam Fawaz Damra, who according to contemporary media reports was known in the Cleveland area "as a voice of moderate, mainstream Islam." He "was often seen at public events with politicians and leaders of other faiths, including several prayer services after the Sept. 11 terrorist attacks." Meanwhile, he was "disparaging Jews in Arabic as 'pigs and monkeys' and raising money for the killing of Jews by the Palestinian Islamic Jihad."

This is just one example of many that confirm the correctness of Ms. Douglass-Williams' observations. Yet despite the reasonableness of her statement, the Canadian Press reports that "there are concerns that Douglass-Williams's views are a hindrance to her work with the foundation and an affront to its legally defined mandate, which is to help eliminate racism and racial discrimination in Canada."

There is in reality no racial issue involved here. Jihad terror and the deceptions of some terror-aligned leaders is not race. Islamic jihadists are people of all races. Ms. Douglass-Williams, in standing against jihad terror and Sharia oppression, is not only not jeopardizing the work of the Canadian Race Relations Foundation, but enhancing it, but standing against the spread of an ideology that is frankly and unapologetically supremacist and violent and set against the survival of Canadian pluralist principles.

Meanwhile, I am deeply concerned that Ms. Douglass-Williams is being smeared by association with me and Jihad Watch. I have been writing against jihad terror and Sharia-justified denial of human rights for many years, and I've found over the years that one tactic that the allies of jihad terror and Sharia supremacist groups frequently resort to in Canada, the U.S., and Western Europe is to smear those who expose their activities as "hatemongers," "racists," and "bigots."

But a false charge does not become true for being often repeated. I invite you to read any of my 17 published books (which I am happy to send you free of charge), thousands of articles, and 45,000+ posts at Jihad Watch, and am confident that you find not a trace of "hatred," "racism," or "bigotry" in them. All my work has been and is in defense of the freedom of speech, the freedom of conscience, and the equality of rights of all people before the law.

More to the point, I invite you to read all of Ms. Douglass-Williams' published writings at Jihad Watch, and you will see that there is no reason for anyone who is concerned about racism and about preserving pluralistic societies to be concerned.

If I can answer any questions or be of any possible service to you in your further consideration of this or any other matter, please do not hesitate to contact me.

> Kindest regards,
>
> Robert Spencer
> Director, Jihad Watch[3]

Dr. Daniel Pipes wrote:

Dear Ms Joly:

I write to express my dismay that you would consider dropping Ms Douglass-Williams from the Canadian Race Relations Foundation board for reasons connected to her views on Islam and related topics.

As the author of a foreword to her very recent book, The Challenge of Modernizing Islam: Reformers Speak Out and The Obstacles They Face, I can assure you that she scrupulously distinguishes between Muslims who uphold Western values and those who are totalitarian.

She is a sophisticated observer of this issue whose knowledge and connections should be of particular value to the foundation - not the reason to force her off the board. Doing so would tarnish CRRF's reputation. I urge you not to.

> Yours sincerely,
>
> Hon. Daniel Pipes
> President
> Middle East Forum[4]

Philanthropist, lawyer and board member of the Centre for Israel and Jewish Affairs, Michael Diamond, stated in a blog:

"I have watched as promise after promise, made in order to get elected, has been avoided or abrogated. I have watched as Trudeau told our veterans, who he promised to assist to improve their situation, were told there was not enough money for them, while enormous amounts are being invested in citizens of other countries brought here as refugees. I have watched as the Liberals eliminated a law introduced by the Conservatives which would have given the government the ability to deport dual citizens who were a security threat to our country. I have recently watched Trudeau welcome former ISIS fighters, who may still be ISIS fighters back into the country, putting ever more strain on the limited resources of our security establishment.

I watched as Islam was elevated above other religions with M-103, in a clearly racist move meant to appease one group of Canadians at the expense of others. I watched as Christine Douglass-Williams was removed as a Director of the Canadian Race Relations Foundation."[5]

I was granted an extension by Melanie Joly to reply to her registered letter. My reply included explanations of the three examples she had identified from my writings.

My response was as follows:

> The extracted passage in Item 1 conveys my concerns about what I termed "Islamic supremacist incursion" into Iceland. There, I characterized Icelanders' "acceptance and tolerance of immigrants" as "admirable" but cautioned about Islamic extremist and terrorist threats against "women, Christians, gays, Jews, apostates, infidels and anyone who dares oppose." Elsewhere, as you will know from my history, I have repeatedly, explicitly indicated that the latter two categories include the great many Muslims who do not bend to extremism. In my recent book, The Challenge of Modernizing Islam, Muslims and others recounted their serious fears about Islamic supremacism and their ideas for doctrinal and other solutions to the much-debated threat of Islamic extremism. In Item 1, I also urged care in accepting at face value exaggerated and divisive claims of racism made by ideological radicals aiming to silence responsible criticism of extremism by cowing those Muslims and non-Muslims who would debate these problems. Various prominent Canadian Muslims have, of course, for many years spoken out about such issues, including author, columnist and former Muslim Canadian Congress member, Raheel Raza, Dr. Farzana Hassan, and University of Western Ontario political-science professor, Dr. Salim Mansur.
>
> No reasonable person could regard this passage, when taken in context, as inconsistent with the duties and responsibilities of a member of the Board of CRRF. Indeed, one would expect no less of a CRRF Board member. As

someone who has condemned publicly every significant variety of extremism and terrorism, whether from neo-Nazi, white, Christian, black, left-fascist, Islamic or other motivation, I could not imagine upon what basis a rational critique of my performance, could be founded.

The same could be said of the content of Item 2.

This Item also warns of what, in Canadian security-and-intelligence terminology, might be referred to as "influence" activity – some of it possibly clandestine in nature and therefore largely unknown to Canadian voters – aimed at deceptively influencing Canada's senators, Members of Parliament and bureaucratic decision-makers, and resultant law and public policy, in favor of radical interests. The passage reflects the responsible view that certain such behavior would be constitutionally untenable, and, consistent with this, unlawful.

The extracted passages under Item 2 convey, in this context, my concerns about the prospect of such troubling influence activity moving Canada toward possible criminalization of the ill-defined, controversial concept of "Islamophobia." Many of Muslim background underscore the fact that, whilst actionable adverse treatment of individual Muslims must be dealt with vigorously under law, the word "Islamophobia" is an unhelpfully ambiguous guide to both law and policy and is misplaced in Motion M103. The incorporating of the root word, "Islam," in this terminology, might suggest that the religion of Islam should be beyond critical discussion in a way that no other religion can or should be held immune to reasonable, Charter, s. 2, free-expression debate.

The content of the third Item quoted my asking rhetorically whether Westerners would "want our cities and countries to become replicas of Islamic states." Taken in context, including my stated concern about "our freedoms and safety," this was a clear in obvious reference to theocratic and theologically dominated states which enforce politico-legal systems that would manifestly be contrary to Canada's Charter of Rights and Freedoms. Jurisdictions operating contrary to Canadian law and values, in this way, would include Iran and Saudi Arabia.

In line with this objection to theologically supremacist governance, whether of Christian, Jewish, Muslim or any other religious dispensation, I proceeded, in the third enumerated Item, to deal with what I described as "the bloodthirsty hatred and evil zeal of Jihadists, who ultimately aim to destroy our freedoms in the name of a religion that is historically rooted in war and conquest." Given the fact that your government is investing vast police and intelligence resources, and considerable funds in "counter-radicalization" programs, all aimed at tamping down the burgeoning threat of Jihad – or "Islamic extremism and terrorism," if you prefer – or other forms of terror and extremism, I cannot imagine that this was intended to be a serious ground of objection to my capacity to serve on the CRRF Board.

## Implications of Joly's Letter and Anti-Islamophobia Motion M-103

Joly's letter and the subsequent mysterious leak to the media had weighty implications. It sent the message, not only to me, but to all Canadians, that Islamic blasphemy laws were to be taken seriously.

Robert Spencer stated of me:

"She opposes jihad terror, and so is under fire on suspicions of "Islamophobia." This is what the Left and Islamic supremacists, as well as the establishment conservatives, have done to Jihad Watch for years, and now the Canadian government of Justin Trudeau is doing the same thing, stigmatizing honest reporting about the nature and magnitude of the jihad terror threat as "bigotry" and "racism."

Meanwhile, who calls Jihad Watch a "hateful website"? A representative of the National Council of Canadian Muslims, formerly known as CAIR-CAN. That's right, HAMAS-linked CAIR. Expect Melanie Joly to jump to do its bidding.

The Left sees its chance after Charlottesville. Leftists are moving rapidly to crush all dissent and destroy all opponents, ripping up the foundations of a free society and demanding that everyone conform to Leftist groupthink, on pain of ostracism (Hillary's "peer pressure and shaming"), character assassination and professional ruin. It's coming down fast. This "scrutiny" of Christine is part of that initiative."[6]

Another report from the Daily Caller expressed concerns about Canada's direction in "inching toward a broadly-based law that would codify 'Islamophobia' as a hate crime without even defining 'Islamophobia' or demonstrating that it is a phenomenon requiring legal action."

The report went on to state that after first passing a motion that condemned Islamophobia, Iqra Khalid, a Member of Parliament from the governing Liberal Party, tabled Motion M-103 in the House of Commons. The motion demanded that 'Islamophobia' be treated as a crime without even bothering to define the offense.[7]

Motion M-103 calls on the government to "condemn Islamophobia and all forms of systemic racism and religious discrimination," asks the government to "recognize the need to quell the increasing public climate of hate and fear," and requests for the "Commons heritage committee to study how the government could develop a government-wide approach to reducing or eliminating systemic racism and religious discrimination, including Islamophobia, and collect data to provide context for hate crime reports and to conduct needs assessments for impacted communities. Findings are to be presented within eight months."[8] Khalid has been "unwilling to entertain any compromise on the specific wording" of Motion 103.[9]

Aside from the National Council of Canadian Muslims (NCCM), there were troubling facts about the other players who were driving M-103. MP Iqra Khalid refused discussion with community members and groups that did not align with her agenda, including those who stressed the need either to fully define "Islamophobia" or change the word in the interests of a united Canada. One of those groups was the Centre for Israel and Jewish Affairs (CIJA), which stated in a declaration that "We believe the term 'Islamophobia' should be replaced with a more precise phrase, such as 'anti-Muslim bigotry,' which was suggested by, among others, former Justice Minister Irwin Cotler."[10]

Khalid sought to use the specifically branded term of "Islamophobia," which is a broad and sweeping term intended to intimidate and silence critics of Islam. Iqra Khalid has a questionable history. She is a former president of the Muslim Brotherhood-linked Muslim Student Association (MSA) at York University. MSA chapters are "essentially an arm of the Saudi-funded, Muslim Brotherhood-controlled Muslim World League." [11] The Muslim Student Association is also well known for its aggressive Boycott, Divestment and Sanctions drives on campus to demonize and delegitimize the State of Israel, and for its members' intimidation of Jewish students.

In January 2016, Khalid received a red-carpet welcome from board members of the Palestine House in Mississauga (near Toronto) and a "large number of members of the Palestinian community," including Palestinian political activists. Palestine House supports the Palestinian al-Quds Intifada, and its settlement program was defunded by the former Conservative Harper government for allying itself with terrorism.[12]

The controversy surrounding Khalid's motion was first portrayed in the mass media as an issue of right versus left and of white supremacists versus "immigrants." Even the tragic shooting in January, 2017 at the Islamic Cultural Centre of Quebec City—in which six people were killed and 19 injured—ended up being used as a political rallying point to shore up support for M-103 and fan the flames of division that were spreading fast, despite the lack of transparency about what really occurred at that mosque and the motive behind the shooting. An exploitative letter to the Prime Minister's Office was sent a year later by the NCCM "to make the anniversary of Quebec City's deadly mosque shooting a day of action on Islamophobia." It was not met with the acceptance that the NCCM expected, as opposition parties in Quebec opposed the request. They

determined that the term 'Islamophobia' to be "too controversial, while the Coalition Avenir Quebec" deemed "the word inappropriate because Quebecers 'are not Islamophobic.' "[13]

Forum Research proved that Canadians widely rejected the 'anti-islamophobia' Motion M-103. The research group found that only 14% of people supported M-103, and an Angus Reid poll showed that only 12% thought that M-103 was "'worth passing' and 'will help reduce anti-Muslim attitudes and discrimination.'"[14]

Behind Khalid's 'anti-Islamophobia' initiative were muscular Muslim Brotherhood lobbies. M-103 was built on petition e-411 by Samer Majzoub, who managed a Muslim Brotherhood-linked Montreal high school and is a leader of the self-described Muslim Brotherhood-linked Muslim Association of Canada (MAC). Majzoub even accused Conservative MPs of "stoking a wave of anti-Muslim sentiment" in opposing M-103.[15]

Petition e-411, which was presented with 70,000 signatures, outlined the contributions of Islam throughout history and declared Islam a religion of peace that had been hijacked by a violent few. The petition was celebrated by the National Council of Canadian Muslims. Its Executive Director, Ihsaan Gardee, said that it sent "a strong message to Canadians that discrimination and hatred against Muslims is unacceptable."[16]

Six major Canadian cities also signed an anti-Islamophobia charter in summer 2017, which was initiated by the NCCM.

As MPs debated Motion M103 in March 2017, 57,731 people signed a petition aimed at MPs and sponsored by Conservative MP James Bezan, calling for an amendment to the Constitution stating that "Sharia Law or separate Sharia family courts will never have a place in the Canadian Justice System." The Canadian Broadcasting Cooperation published an article entitled: *Sharia and rules that govern religious practices in other faiths are not to be feared, spiritual leaders say."*[17]

The gist of the article was that shariah was already in Canada and that peaceful, devout Muslims who practiced it were merely exercising their right to faith, like any other faith; therefore, shariah was harmless. The article did not mention the fact that shariah is very different in practice, as is evident in Islamic states globally and as is clear from Islamic fiqh and the major schools of Sunni and Shia jurisprudence. Shariah is Islamic law, which all Muslims are obligated to obey. Shariah encompasses a supremacist legal system, is regarded as divine law above every other law, allows a man to have up to four wives, and mandates certain punishments deemed contrary to human rights and Canadian laws—including amputation, beheading, flogging, and the killing of adulterers, apostates, and gays as well as wife-beating. It also orders that women be covered up:

> *(Quran 24:31) And tell the believing women to reduce of their vision and guard their private parts and not expose their adornment except that which appears thereof and to wrap [a portion of] their headcovers over their chests and not expose their adornment except to their husbands, their fathers, their husbands' fathers, their sons, their husbands' sons, their brothers, their brothers' sons, their sisters' sons, their women, that which their right hands possess, or those male attendants having no physical desire, or children who are not yet aware of the private aspects of women. And let them not stamp their feet to make known what they conceal of their adornment. And turn to Allah in repentance, all of you, O believers, that you might succeed.*

If a woman does not cover, she is fair game to be assaulted:

> *(Quran 33:59) O Prophet, tell your wives and your daughters and the women of the believers to bring down over themselves of their outer garments. That is more suitable that they will be known and not be abused.*

At least 85 shariah courts are operational in the UK. They were originally intended to resolve family, marriage, and financial disputes for Muslims, but they are misogynistic and consequently damaging to women, and by proxy to children. Shariah-compliant women (or women under control of shariah-compliant men) are subjugated and intimidated, while Muslim men are commanded by the Qur'an to beat wives from whom they merely suspect disobedience and need simply to tell their wives "I divorce you" three times to be free of them. Many women in Britain's shariah courts are being sent back to severely abusive, life-threatening spousal relationships.[18]

Shariah is not harmless to Canada, and neither is Motion M-103.

A series of Canadian Race Relations Foundation meetings and orientation sessions, which welcomed new board members selected by the Department of Heritage, was set for October 10-17, 2017. As a member of the Executive Committee, I attended these orientations, as well as committee meetings and board meetings. It was a most pleasant time. I was personally told by the Chairman that the situation looked settled, so that my appointment would likely play out until the following May. This seemed plausible, given that I had not been contacted by Joly or the Privy Council Office.

Regular email contact between Executive Committee members and the Investment Committee duties continued as usual right up until mid-December 2017, when I participated in a Skype meeting with the Executive team, with an agenda of moving the CRRF forward with new board members and the vision for the CRRF.

A week later, on December 20, 2017 at 3:50pm, while en route for our family holiday, I received an email out of the blue that read:

*Dear Ms. Douglass-Williams,*

*Please find attached an Order in Council terminating your appointment as a director of the Board of Directors of the Canadian Race Relations Foundation, effective December 19, 2017. The Order in Council will be posted on the Privy Council Office website in the next several days.*

*Sincerely,*

*Janine Sherman*
*Deputy Secretary to the Cabinet*

My immediate reaction was one of pure sadness. To be accused of being anti-Muslim, intolerant, and out of sync with the mission of the CRRF was unjust, wrong, even slanderous. As a patriotic Canadian who ardently advances equality and human rights for all, and freedom of religion—if practiced within the limits of Western democratic rights and freedoms—did not make me an "Islamophobic" fiend.

It also emerged the next day in the *Toronto Star* that the National Council of Canadian Muslims had "expressed concerns and sent a formal letter to the government in October. Executive director Ihsaan Gardee said Douglass-Williams' removal is an 'appropriate corrective measure taken by government to address (her) disturbing public record.' "

The NCCM/CAIR-CAN, like its parent CAIR in America, is found any and everywhere the word "Islamophobia" is used and abused. It was not surprising to find this group advising and influencing the Liberal government of Canada. If anything was disturbing, it was that the influence of an unindicted co-conspirator to the 2008 Holy Land Foundation HAMAS terror financing trial was implicated in my termination from the CRRF. It did not help my case either that Muslim Member of Parliament Arif Virani was Parliamentary Secretary to Melanie Joly and was solidly defending M-103.

Virani came to Canada as a Ugandan refugee and has blamed the Conservatives for being intolerant and taking a "hardline" approach to the niqab, yet in many African countries, such as Chad, Gabon, Congo, Morocco, and parts of Cameroon, the niqab has been banned for security reasons. Virani also has a personal impulse to teach Canadians what Islam is all about. He stated:

> "I think it's both a responsibility but also a duty, that as Islamic members of Parliament now we really need to be in the vanguard of carrying forward a mantle that demonstrates to all Canadians, not just to our constituents in our individual ridings, about what our religion is about and what Canadian people are really about."[19]

**M**y firing was widely publicized the following day. Concerns and questions poured in about how anyone could be fired for criticizing Islam, jihad, Islamic supremacism, the Muslim Brotherhood, and shariah and its abuses. I was encouraged by the outpouring of support, but also disturbed about the direction the Liberal government was taking in Canada. It had made a public and clear statement to me and to Canada that it would not tolerate criticism of Islam, as per M-103.

Robert Spencer wrote:

It is unconscionable that Christine Douglass-Williams has been dismissed from the Canadian Race Relations Foundation for calling attention to the reality of jihad terror. Whether the Canadian government likes it or not, and however it stigmatizes and attempts to marginalize honest discussion of these issues, jihad terror is a grim reality and they will not be able to avoid it or deny it forever. Canada, by dismissing Ms. Douglass-Williams for writing for Jihad Watch, is buying into the notion that it is offensive and wrong to track, publicize, and oppose jihad terror and shariah supremacist activity. Once we are all silenced, the jihad will be able to advance unopposed and unimpeded. Apparently, that is what Mr. Trudeau and Ms. Joly want.[20]

Writer Daniel Greenfield stated in Frontpage Magazine:

Real racism is the racism that no one dares to speak out against. It's the racism that is accepted as the established norm. It's the racism that you are punished for speaking out against,

As Christine Douglass-Williams was.

*"I have been terminated from the Canadian Race Relations Foundation, four months after a threatening letter by Heritage Minister Melanie Joly about my writings on Islam at Jihad Watch.*

*Joly made good on her threats. The Privy Council has terminated my appointment, despite my years of dedicated commitment to the Foundation, on which I also served as Chair of the Investment Committee, and as a member of the Human Resource and Executive Committees. Why? Because I dared to criticize political Islam on Jihad Watch. ..."*

So the Canadian government has fired an anti-racism activist for criticizing a supremacist racist organization. It's just one that happens to be protected by the left.[21]

Tom Quiggin, a former military intelligence officer and a court appointed expert on jihadist terrorism, wrote:

Douglass-Williams' firing is worrying as it emanates from the Canadian Heritage Ministry – the same ministry which is holding hearings into the anti-Islamophobia Motion M-103. This motion was entered into the Parliament by Iqra Khalid. This is noteworthy, as Member of Parliament Iqra Khalid claims to have written the Constitution for the York University Muslim Student Association. The constitution of the York University MSA states that it is Salafist in orientation and supports shariah Law.

This firing does not occur in isolation. It has been revealed that ISIS fighters returning to Canada have not had their names put forward to the UN committee for the list of international jihadists. Furthermore, Prime Minister Trudeau has stated that terrorist travelers from ISIS can be "an extraordinarily powerful voice" for deradicalization. Prime Minister Trudeau also states that "we have methods of de-emphasizing or de-programming people who want to harm our society." This claim despite the fact that the Canadian government's leaderless Centre for Community Engagement and Prevention of Violence does not have a deradicalization program, nor is there any such "bricks and mortar" center in Canada. Furthermore, Canada appears to lack any law that could force the ISIS fighters to attend a program if it existed. France, by example, just sponsored a similar program which was a total failure....

The firing of Christine Douglass-Williams should be seen in a specific context. Canada has an Islamic supremacist entryist problem in government. The Prime Minister has addressed a gathering of Muslim Brotherhood linked groups in Canada and told them that he shared their beliefs, values, and vision. The Prime Minister also says that returning ISIS fighters can be a "powerful voice" while the government does not have a deradicalization program and ISIS fighter's names are not added to the list of international jihadists. Trudeau demonstrated his greatest show of passion ever in parliament as he defended ISIS fighters, when confronted by opposition leader Andrew Scheer over ISIS fighters returning to Canada.[22]

# PART 2

---

## THE USE OF VICTIMOLOGY AND IDENTITY POLITICS BY CIVILIZATIONAL JIHADISTS

### Preamble

The second part of this document explores the important concept of victimology as a role played in identity politics that influences the direction of multicultural societies in major spheres of: immigration management, individual freedoms, group identity, and ultimately homeland security. The major thrust of this section is that Islamic supremacist groups such as the Muslim Brotherhood have exploited victimology in their manipulation of multiculturalism, the anti-racism industry, diversity drives, Muslim populations, and the socialist-left leadership of many Western nations.

It is important to grasp that keeping people oppressed or otherwise "helping" them to embrace an identity of oppression enables totalitarian agendas. Some points to note about this modus operandi: i) education among "oppressed" groups is discouraged, as knowledge enlightens. Because knowledge is empowering, the oppressor's power is diminished as the oppressed becomes enlightened. ii) oppressed groups can be manipulated to revolution in support of their corrupt leaders' indoctrinated vision, ideology, and goals. iii) oppressed populations are relatively easy to control via leadership propaganda, due to their lack of education, their poverty, and dependence on their corrupt, but venerated leaders. Oppressed populations also permit a convenient enlarging of power distances between them and their leaders, so that their leaders lead, and they follow in obedient trust, whether or not those leaders are worthy of that trust.

In Western societies, two phenomena can be observed among the united socialist left, which benefits the victimology narrative: the first is a bigotry of low expectations, which instills the detrimental idea that brown people and black people are to be pitied forever because they have been nearly irreparably broken by white people. They are therefore deemed to be at least partially justified in any unlawful or harmful act they commit of which the same behavior is regarded as unacceptable in white society. Embedded in this lenience of expectation toward brown and black people is a presumption of their inferiority, although it is never presented that way. For example, it is overlooked that Arabs hold black slaves, that women are sold into sex slavery by Muslims, that child brides are being sentenced to torturous marriages in Islam. In this view, ethnic people do not need to abide by the same rules of human rights that white people are expected to observe because they are deemed to be inept, incapable of overcoming and of achieving.

In this view, it is peculiar that it is generally unrecognized—or at least seldom articulated—that Islam has been engaging in such practices for 1400 years, because one need look no further than the white man. It is always and must always be the white man's fault to maintain the very status quo that its enablers pretend to reject: *i.e.*, the bigotry of low expectations. The same victimhood mentality applies to blacks. Although there are significant differences in the history of non-Muslim blacks and Muslims, and reasons why these groups retain the status of oppressed groups, the reasons put forth by their socialist and Islamic supremacist leaders are: white privilege, white oppression, white supremacy. All the while, when members of these groups victimize others, it is ignored. The victimization within these groups is also ignored.

Secondly, this system allows for a guarantee that leaders of the publicly and privately funded "anti-racism" industry are well-off, while their client "victims" remain ghettoized.

Of course, there are those in the anti-racism industry who are sincere, who assist in the healing of past wounds, who aid in the practicalities of individual and group development, and who cultivate unity, true diversity, pluralism, and a strong national identity, but these represent a struggling minority within the industry.

The anti-racism industry as a whole has been hijacked by powerful, known lobbies such as Muslim Brotherhood offshoots and Black Lives Matter, in which those two lobbies have now managed to converge.

The victimhood status quo also enables the expansion of a totalitarian agenda, in which big government is needed to "help" the people who are unable to help themselves. In this scenario, selling "compassion" for the so-called oppressed is a marketing tool, whereby "experts" and government political leaders line their pockets as the self-proclaimed protectors of the wretchedly oppressed.

In this scenario, there must be a villain, *i.e.*, the group doing the oppressing and this group must be controlled, silenced or both. This villainous group constitutes the specter of the masters of oppression from the days of colonialism and slavery. Their victims regrettably remain in shackles, the cycle of the bigotry of low expectations continues, and the oppressed remain stunted.

Western societies have evolved to become diverse and immigrant-friendly. This is not to say that racism, intolerance, xenophobia, and bigotry do not exist. They do, but they are not exclusive to white people but are also found among various groups of immigrants.

Western constitutions permit all citizens to scrutinize and criticize government and various ideologies, to dialogue and debate openly, and to hold one another accountable. This makes for the continuance and preservation of democratic freedoms. The hallmark of democracy is freedom of speech, while totalitarianism is marked by little to no freedom of expression. It is the duty of elected government representatives to protect and serve the people that elected them, not to betray their constituencies and serve their own personal agendas, or worse, foreign political agendas. Hate laws were created in Canada with the noble intent to protect all groups of people equally, not ideologies. Such laws were not deemed to be laws of privilege but to protect all Canadian citizens against intended public incitement of hatred and willful promotion of hatred.

Within the criminal code, a provision states that one must not be convicted of a hate crime if: i) the statements communicated are true, ii) "if, in good faith, the person expressed or attempted to establish by an argument an opinion on a religious subject or an opinion based on a belief in a religious text; or iii) if "the statements were relevant to any subject of public interest, the discussion of which was for the public benefit, and if on reasonable grounds he believed them to be true." Under the Liberal Government of Canada, hate laws have evolved to encompass identity politics in which truthful discussions about the global jihad and barbaric cultural practices are being wrongly presented as though they were inciting hatred, "racist" and hateful. The next section elaborates upon the severity and implications of this crisis Canada is now in. [23]

# CANADA'S M-103 FOLLOW-UP

On June 1, 2018, The Liberal Government released a document titled: "Government Response to the Tenth Report of the Standing Committee on Canadian Heritage Entitled: Taking Action Against Systemic Racism and Religious Discrimination Including Islamophobia."[24]

Signed by Melanie Joly and addressed to Julie Dabrusin, Chair of the Standing Committee on Canadian Heritage, this document was a follow-up document to anti-Islamophobia Motion M-103. As with M-103, the document was not presented as a singular "anti-islamophobia" document, but as an all-inclusive package to fight "racism," "discrimination," and "islamophobia."[25]

Absent from this document, as expected, was a legitimate and concrete definition of "islamophobia," so "islamophobia" was incorporated into the document as a form of racism and discrimination. "Islamophobia" was singled out as a problematic phenomenon in Canada that victimized Muslims, and that needs special attention.

Most Canadians will agree that racism, discrimination, and intolerance are not welcome in Canada, but "Islamophobia" remains undefined in Canadian law, although it is well-defined in Islamic states that are governed by the shariah. Shariah forbids any criticism of Islam, and the Organization of Islamic Cooperation (OIC), which works to enforce this anti-blasphemy rule globally, has installed a special "Islamophobia Observatory" to do so.

This OIC agenda is now being promulgated by the current Canadian Liberal government, in its foisting of the "Islamophobia" agenda upon all Canadians. From here on, I will focus on the problematic "Islamophobia" component of the Standing Committee on Canadian Heritage document and on what particular "action" the government intends to implement to combat "Islamophobia."

While delivering testimony before M-103 Committee hearings in October 2017, celebrated human rights lawyer David Matas urged Members of Parliament "to be careful in their use of the term Islamophobia," saying "fear of some elements of Islam is mere prudence."[26]

So, is the government of Canada calling this prudent concern about elements of Islam "racist" and "discriminatory"? Evidently, yes.

As a follow-up, the Government of Canada has now vowed to "take action" against those whom it deems to be exhibiting "Islamophobia." But what does this 'action' really mean? For starters:  $23 million of taxpayer money was designated by the Liberal Government over two years to provide increased funds for the Multiculturalism Program administered by Canadian Heritage, with fighting "Islamophobia" included.[27]

Iqra Khalid held a press conference at the end of June 2018, in which she openly admitted that CAIR-CAN/NCCM and IRFAN (International Relief Fund for the Afflicted and Needy Canada) will be receiving funds from the $23-million. Khalid boldly stated:

> *We don't need support as Canadians, we need a foundation and that is what the government is doing with this funding, with these $23 million that will go a long way toward helping organizations like The Boys and Girls Club. ... NCCM that does a lot of data collecting on hate crimes and pushing that advocacy needle forward in our country or like Islamic Relief ... that does not only work within Canada, across Canada but across the world in removing those stereotypes and there are so many more ...."[28]*

The CAIR-CAIR/CAN-NCCM connection has already been mentioned. Here is more concerning information, this time regarding IRFAN and the Muslim Association of Canada (MAC).

In 2015, it was uncovered that an RCMP search warrant linked the MAC headquarters in Mississauga (near Toronto) to IRFAN, which was designated as a banned terrorist organization by the Conservative Stephen Harper government in 2014.[29] Although no charges were laid by the RCMP, a Canada Revenue Agency document showed that "MAC provided $296,514 between 2001 and 2010" to IRFAN-Canada.[30] Within that period, from 2005 to 2009, "IRFAN-Canada transferred approximately $14.6 million worth of resources to various organizations associated with HAMAS," according to the federal department of public safety. [31]

In revisiting the debate surrounding the introduction of Motion M-103, its proponents frequently argued that the motion was not law, but a benign motion that would be passed in Parliament for further study by the Heritage Committee. It subsequently proved to be as dangerous as opponents had warned. Now, action against "Islamophobia" has bypassed the legislature to be fully incorporated into a government "action" plan that would affect multiple divisions of Canadian society, identified in the document as "themes." These "themes" include: Federal Action, Indigenous Affairs, Education and Awareness, Data and Evidence, and Law Enforcement.[32]

Some critical indications with respect to "Islamophobia" referenced in Joly's document:

1. Government action is required to counter the effects of Islamophobia. Such action "will include programs and policies with a whole of government approach." As such, funding will go to activities to "create conversations about Muslims, the impact of Islamophobia."[33]

2. As part of the "Islamophobia" initiative, Canadian citizens will be **monitored for compliance**: the Public Service Commission of Canada "offers standardized assessment instruments through its Personnel Psychology Center for use by public service organizations." These tests are developed with "diverse groups and are monitored and maintained with diversity in mind."[34]

It has already been established that among these groups (as Iqra Khalid mentioned) will be the NCCM and IRFAN. According to the NCCM website, the organization also provides education (aka indoctrination) to "government departments, law enforcement officers, media agencies, and private organizations," through workshops and "full day Bootcamps."[35]

3. Support for initiatives that "promote interfaith and intercultural dialogue in the Education and Awareness part of the document" is included, and "Islamophobia" is specified. An example was also provided in the document of a past round table discussion event that was hosted by the Parliamentary Secretary Omar Alghabra, whose disturbing background will be addressed later on.[36]

4. The recognition of hate crimes is "captured in the Criminal Code of Canada," specifically Sections 318 and 319. Section 318: Hate Propaganda, refers specifically to advocating for genocide. Section 319: Public incitement of hatred, refers to stirring up hatred in a public place. With respect to Section 218 and 319, the "Government of Canada also recognizes that the effectiveness of these hate speech laws requires law enforcement agencies to have training, preparedness, and capacity to report and investigate hate crimes, both offline and in the cyber domain."[37]

With the "Islamophobia" subterfuge now woven into Canada's multiculturalism, and with the government vowing "action" against those it deems to be guilty of "Islamophobia," significant resources may well be allocated to witch-hunts by law enforcement agencies to silence free speech when it is deemed offensive to Islam. For example, in Joly's document, the Government's plan of action to advance its version of media literacy with respect to cultural and interfaith awareness, includes what it defines as "fake news" and "hate speech." Disturbingly, the government's intention of cracking down on "far right" groups, along with "Daesh" was also specifically included.[38]

While Daesh (aka the Islamic State) was mentioned, the government did not define what it meant by "far right" groups. It avoided a clear and concise definition and identification of "far right," just as it avoided a definition of "Islamophobia."

> 5. Joly's document also focuses upon the January 29, 2017 "terrorist attack on worshippers at the Islamic Cultural Center in Quebec City," which was indeed a horrible tragedy, but was found by a court not to be a terrorist attack.

Of noted concern is that the Trudeau government also exhibited "totalitarian tendencies" in its Canada Summer Jobs program, according to the former head of the Office of Religious Freedom, Dr. Andrew Bennett.[39] Action was taken by the Trudeau government to shut down summer job grants for any organization that did not agree to support abortion rights, thus eliminating Christian organizations, regardless of the nature of their business.

Meanwhile, the Muslim Association of Canada was approved to receive grants to fund activities for its various Ontario chapters,[40] as was the Islamic Humanitarian Service, whose director Shafiq Hudda once called for the "eradication of Israelis" and proclaimed that he wanted to see "Israelis in body bags."[41]

When pressed during Question Period in the House of Commons, Trudeau refused to acknowledge the persecution of Christians in the Middle East and to recognize that Christians were victims of Daesh/ISIS. All the while, Trudeau has referred to evangelical Christians as the "worst part of Canadian society," according to a first-hand account by Pastor Steve Long, a Canadian Baptist Minister.[42]

**Opposition Conservative Government's Rejected Minority Report**

The opposition Conservative government provided an alternative minority report to M-103, which was rejected by Melanie Joly's department in her latest document. Here is an excerpt from the "Conservative Party Of Canada – Minority Report of the Standing Committee on Canadian Heritage on Systemic Racism and Religious Discrimination":[43]

*"The debate on M-103 captured the attention of Canadians and the mainstream media for several weeks. The main objection Canadians had to M-103 was that it complicated and confused the issue of anti-Muslim bigotry and violence rather than clarified it.*

*The word 'Islamophobia,' which features prominently in M-103, has a long history. Unfortunately, 'Islamophobia' has received many definitions, and the failure to use just one definition for the word is highly problematic.*

*We believed that the motion would have better achieved its goal by condemning "all forms of systemic racism, religious intolerance, and discrimination of Muslims, Jews, Christians, Sikhs, Hindus, and other religious communities."*

*Our amendment to this effect was rejected by the Liberals, who then voted to pass M-103. The public reaction to this by Canadians, both inside and outside of the Muslim community, was one of widespread concern that the issue was being politicized in a way that was limiting healthy debate rather than encouraging it......*

*AN INCREASING PUBLIC CLIMATE OF HATE AND FEAR"*

*M-103 begins with the assertion that Canada is experiencing an "increasing public climate of hate and fear"and that it is the Government of Canada's responsibility to "quell" such a phenomenon. However, witness testimony and Statistics Canada data suggests that this assumption does not fully reflect reality.*

*Dr. Sherif Emil, pediatric surgeon at the Montreal Children's Hospital, was clear with Committee members about his experience as a visible minority Canadian:*

*"If systemic racism and religious discrimination existed, I probably wouldn't be a pediatric surgeon today...Nobody had ever asked me in my training, in my selection, who I was or what I believed in. No, I do not believe systemic racism and discrimination exists. I believe discrimination and racism exists. It existed in many circumstances, it exists in many situations and that's totally unfortunate, but I don't think it's systemic. ...* [44]

The Conservative Government Minority Report was reasonable. It incorporated the rejection of bigotry, intolerance, and racism. It took into consideration the proud progress of Canada, while protecting the principles of equality, human rights, pluralism, and democracy itself.

With the strength of Islamic supremacist influence in the Liberal government, and its declared determination to act against "Islamophobia," Motion M-103 threatens Canada's democratic freedoms, of which freedom of expression is the cornerstone. It also places shariah principles, which mandate punishments for criticizing Islam, as a new cornerstone, given the special privileges now bestowed upon Muslims above every other faith and doctrine. Given Canada's added problem of having a Prime Minister who welcomes any and everyone into the country, including Islamic State jihadis, America will have to contend with a weak link in its own security.

The Organization of Islamic Cooperation (OIC) maintains an Observatory on "Islamophobia," which it claims to be a human rights issue. The OIC rejected the UN Declaration of Human Rights in 1990 and pledged to the Cairo Declaration of Human Rights in Islam, under which the only human rights recognized by the Islamic governments of the world are those allowed under the shariah. The OIC has been relentless in keeping "Islamophobia" on the agenda of international relations and in advocating for a common strategy to defeat those whom it deems to be fomenting hate against Muslims.

Article 24 of the Cairo Declaration of Human Rights states that "All the rights and freedoms stipulated in this Declaration are subject to the Islamic Shari'ah." Article 25 states that "the Islamic Shari'ah is the only source of reference for the explanation or clarification of any of the articles of this Declaration."[45]

In April 1999, the United Nations Commission on Human Rights (now the UN Human Rights Council) adopted a resolution against "Defamation of Religions" introduced by Pakistan—the country widely known for its cruel blasphemy laws—on behalf of the Organization of the Islamic Conference (later renamed Organization of Islamic Cooperation) that purported to be concerned with "negative stereotyping of religions," particularly in Western countries; it condemned Western free speech for its criticism of Islam.[46]

In the resolution, the UN Commission on Human Rights expressed "deep concern at negative stereotyping of religions and manifestations of intolerance in some regions of the world, and the frequent and wrong association of Islam with human rights violations and terrorism."[47]

"Following a republication of the Danish Mohammed cartoons, OIC Secretary General Ekmeleddin Ihsanoglu called them 'blasphemous' and declared that 'these misguided Islamophobic acts, by deeply hurting the feelings of one-fifth of humanity, go beyond the freedom of expression or press."[48]

UN Resolution 16/18 in 2011 continued to advance the substance of the Defamation of Religions Resolution. Paragraph 5 (e) of Resolution 16/18 identifies a need for "Speaking out against intolerance, including advocacy of religious hatred that constitutes incitement to discrimination, hostility or violence."[49]

At an OIC-led meeting, where nations attacked the West for associating Islam with terrorism, Ambassador Ömür Orhun—Permanent Representative of Turkey to The Organization for Security and Co-operation in Europe—rebuked the use of the term "Islamic terrorism" by the Western media following terrorist attacks and affirmed that "there is no such thing as Islamic terrorism."[50]

The OIC has been the world's foremost leader in cracking down on the view that Islam is in any way associated with human rights violations and with terrorism, even though there is an association.[51] This strategy to combat defamation of Islam has been forcefully advanced by the OIC internationally, as well as by the UN General Assembly and it is leading to the usurping of democracies through a highly advanced network of Muslim establishments.

What we see is a hijacking by the OIC of the Western principle of the freedom of speech, as it boldly attempts to impose shariah blasphemy/slander laws on free societies. M-103 is an offshoot of this drive.

The Trudeau government sent a delegation to the 44th session of the Council of Foreign Ministers of the Organization of Islamic Cooperation. Canada was represented by the Liberal parliamentary Secretary For Foreign Affairs, Saudi-born Omar Alghabra, whose parents are Syrian.

Alghabra has a disturbing history:

- Omar Alghabra was described by Al Jazeera as a "long-time personal friend of Trudeau" who was at the Liberal leadership convention when Trudeau won. Alghabra commented after the win that "the results were overwhelmingly joyful...It was really incredible to see the results of the hard work come to an end." Al Jazeera commented that it was "an achievement the Syrian-Canadian can take some credit for." In that same article, Alghabra commended Trudeau's vision to engage with Iran and told Al Jazeera: "On the issue of Iran, Trudeau has clearly stated that he is for engagement." Alghabra also credited Trudeau with having values "in sync" with his own.[52]

- In 2013, Alghabra criticized the Harper government's decision to cancel relief money sent to Syria via Human Concern International (HCI), which has offices in Beirut, Somalia and Pakistan.[53] HCI was also investigated by U.S. officials, and under the Jean Chretien government in 1997, funding was cut off from HCI, for what official documents called "the group's terrorism connections."[54] Then in 2015, the RCMP listed HCI in a terrorism investigation search warrant, when tax records showed that HCI granted $68,820 to the International Relief Fund for the Afflicted and Needy (IRFAN) between 2005 and 2009.[55]An RCMP wiretap also revealed that "the user of the Montreal IRFAN telephone number ... was in contact with HCI office in Montreal in October 2013 and December 2013."[56] IRFAN was declared a terrorist group by the Harper government in April 2014 for transferring approximately $14.6 million dollars to charities associated with HAMAS.[57] The HAMAS charter calls for the obliteration of Israel.

- Alghabra served as President of the Canadian Arab Federation in 2004, a group that once "issued a press release entitled Listing of terrorist organizations must be put in perspective which opposes the designation of HAMAS and Palestinian Islamic Jihad as terrorist entities by the Government of Canada."[58]

- In 2014, a federal court upheld the government's decision to end funding to the Canadian Arab Federation over its support for terrorist organizations.[59] 74% of a CAF budget for training new immigrants was from taxpayers.[60] The Citizenship and Immigration Minister at the time was Jason Kenney, who "described the CAF as 'radical and anti-semitic' [sic] and called the funding arrangement 'shameful.'"[61] Noted was a comment made by the CEO of the Center for Israel and Jewish Affairs (CIJA), Shimon Fogel:
  > "It's particularly disturbing to think that an organization that holds views so diametrically opposed to Canada's values was given a mandate to integrate new Canadians."[62]

- During Alghabra's term as President of the CAF, he slammed the National Post report that referred to the Al-Aqsa Brigade as a "terrorist group," and stated: "CanWest, one of the largest media conglomerates in Canada, is failing its responsibility towards all Canadians, not just Arabs and Muslims."[63]

- Also during his term as CAF president, Alghabra wrote to Toronto police chief Bill Blair to protest Blair's decision to lead a "Walk for Israel."[64]

- In the letter, which was posted on CAF's website, Alghabra called Israel *"a country that is conducting a brutal and the longest contemporary military occupation in the world. This event coupled with your recent participation in a delegation of police chiefs that went on a six-day trip to Israel on March 1, has begun to create a feeling of genuine distrust and confusion for what appears to be your public endorsement of the practices of the state of Israel."*[65]

- On January 5, 2006, Alghabra told the Jewish Tribute: "I don't believe that HAMAS wants the elimination of Israel."[66] Alghabra should know what is in the HAMAS Charter. The Tribune article also stated that Alghabra "told the Jewish Tribune that he has 'always spoken out against extremism and violence against civilians'. But when asked whether he would specifically denounce suicide bombers, he would not comment, claiming that he was being 'trapped.'"[67] Upon the death of one of the worst jihad terrorists ever, Yasser Arafat, "Alghabra's CAF put out a press release mourning the terrorist's death with 'sorrow and regret.'" The release stated:

    *"This is a time of reflection and reaffirmation of commitment to the Palestinian just cause of struggle for freedom and self-determination."*[68]

- At the 38th Parliament, 1st Session's Subcommittee on Public Safety and National Security of the Standing Committee on Justice, Human Rights, Public Safety and Emergency Preparedness, Alghabra opposed an anti-terrorist act brought forward by Liberal Prime Minister Paul Martin. As leader of the CAF, he stated:

    *"Our concern then as community members was that the Anti-terrorism Act was the wrong response to the events of September 11, 2001. I'll tell you why it's wrong. It's wrong because it trades fundamental Canadian values, such as the rule of law, respect for human dignity, and fairness, to gain a false sense of security. It's wrong because it's motivated and conceived out of fear."*[69]

- Alghabra also reportedly said that "he was disappointed Ontario's decision not to adopt Sharia Islamic law for Muslim divorces during a 2003-2006 debate, calling the move not to take on Muslim law in Canada 'unfortunate.'"[70]

In a troubling report, B'nai Brith Canada drew attention to an official guidebook published by the Toronto District School Board that condemned "Islamophobia" and defined the term to include "***dislike directed ... towards Islamic politics or culture.***[71] This guidebook was prepared with the support of the National Council of Canadian Muslims, which strongly campaigned for

M-103 and was influential in setting up 'Islamophobia Charters' in six Canadian cities.

Michael Mostyn, CEO of B'nai Brith Canada, wrote in the National Post: "To be clear, banning or even discouraging any 'dislike' of 'Islamic politics' would make it nearly impossible to combat the virulent Jew-hatred that we have seen emanating from some Muslim institutions in Canada."[72]

The motive of stealth jihadists is to advance an expansionary agenda. The Muslim Brotherhood has recognized a mammoth opportunity to exploit the anti-racism industry in every sector of Western society by utilizing participants of the industry as human shields to protect the advancement of its doctrine. While free speech is the cornerstone of democracy, silencing criticism of Islam is the cornerstone of shariah.

Stealth jihadists have entwined the criticism of Islam and racism together so cleverly that the two variables are indistinguishable to a significant segment of Western populations, which are eager to be welcoming. In this formula, one cannot criticize Islam without being "racist," and one cannot oppose racism without including "Islamophobia."

The Muslim Brotherhood has managed to form an opportunistic partnership with the leaders of victimology-promoting groups and individuals, where the maintenance of the oppressed identity is extolled. Oppressed identities must have an oppressor. To these groups, it is white society that is the oppressor while visible minorities who do not agree are completely ignored and/or regarded to be traitors to the "oppressed" group. Western guilt for past wrongs only adds to this dilemma.

In an exclusive report, the Investigative Project for Terrorism revealed that the far left Southern Poverty Law Center (SPLC) hired a public relation firm to help them compile their *"Field Guide to Anti-Muslim Extremists."* This firm employed former Council on American Islamic Relations (CAIR) officials.[73] The SPLC is well known for slandering those who warn about the well-documented civilizational jihad by labeling them as "Islamophobes."

## ANTI-RACISM, MULTICULTURALISM AND THE DESTABILIZATION OF WESTERN DEMOCRACY

The anti-racism industry perpetuates an us-versus-them narrative of victimhood as it fosters hate and helplessness among those deemed by them to be oppressed. This inevitably provides motives for harm perpetrated by visible minorities against white members of society. The industry discourages use of the term "visible minority," despite the terminology becoming an acceptable template among all members of society to describe the non-white sector of the population. To them, every word is scrutinized for offence, so that society must walk on eggshells to appease the taskmasters of political correctness. In this nerve-wracking climate, there can be no freedom to pursue genuine dialogue, pluralism, and freedom of speech, because only one side of the equation is privileged: those deemed to be "oppressed."

From the beginning of recorded history, the enslavement and abuse of peoples existed. Yet, in modern times, Western-style democracy is the only system globally that attracts vast numbers of immigrants of every race and creed. Democratic constitutions protect human rights and allow for equal rights, freedom of religion, and freedom of expression.

There was once an era in which the visible minority immigration was not a part of the norm in Europe and the Americas. During the post-slavery era, the biggest challenge was the integration of blacks into the mainstream white society, which was not an easy task. The tragic mindset that held blacks to be lesser human beings was endemic.

It was to be expected that there would be a difficult period of growth following emancipation. Victims must own the reality of their abuse, but once they are free, they must own the reality of their freedom.

Frederick Douglass, the 19th-century abolitionist, human rights leader, author, orator and the first African American to hold a high U.S. government rank, was born into slavery. He knew firsthand the stench of racism and abuse that was based on a person's skin color. In 1865, the same year America abolished slavery and the immediate challenge of emancipation—physically, psychologically, and economically—was most urgent, Douglass eschewed the continuation of the view that blacks were inferior and in need of special care and privilege to advance themselves.[74]

At this stage, one could legitimately argue that Douglass' expectations were too high under the circumstances and that he added to the burden of blacks who had already been stripped of their dignity and humanity. Douglass stated:

"Everybody has asked the question 'What shall we do with the Negro?' I have had but one answer from the beginning. Do nothing with us!" He added, "If the apples will not remain on the tree of their own strength, if they are worm-eaten at the core, if they are early ripe and disposed to fall, let them fall! I am not for tying or fastening them on the tree in any way, except by nature's plan, and if they will not stay there, let them fall. And if the Negro cannot stand on his own legs, let him fall also. All I ask is, give him a chance to stand on his own legs! Let him alone!"[75]

Core to Douglass' philosophy was equality between races. He believed that blacks could overcome abuse by joining together and supporting one another. He did not reject the help of white people, but he did reject the pitying of blacks and their assignment to victimhood. One can see such a positive example in the Jews who survived the Holocaust.

Many black leaders have fostered rage and nurtured the belief that blacks need special privilege because in their view, whites have had it too good for too long. Such leaders do not take into consideration the successes of their own black community; instead, they focus on past white sins and blame the failure within their own communities on whites. Worst yet is that they ignore the fact that Muslim Arabs are still denigrating blacks and even holding black slaves in Mauritania, Sudan, and Algeria. [Muslims *are* blacks all over the world, although granted, there is an Arab hauteur within Islam, it having originated on the Arabian Peninsula.]

Racism, discrimination, intolerance, and bigotry are as old as poverty, and while it is necessary to continue progressing and striving against intolerance, the West has evolved into a bastion of human rights. The West has become fully multicultural, not necessarily in terms of adopting multicultural legislation, but in terms of demographic makeup.

The Japanese have survived the persecution and abuse of the Chinese and moved on, and Jews who survived the brutality of the Holocaust also moved on, but the black community continues to suffer a scourge of black-on-black violence, low education statistics, and one-parent households, not just in white countries, but also in predominantly black countries. The assignment of permanent victimhood and pity is damaging.

## Victimhood Indoctrination as a Home-Base for Revolution

Following its first black presidency, America is more polarized than ever. Rather than celebrate the advancement of blacks while continuing to progress toward unity and peaceful dialogue, along comes the Black Lives Matter Movement to foment violence against the front-line protectors of our societies."[76]

Nation of Islam leader Louis Farrakhan indoctrinates hatred against police into his followers using cases of blacks who have been killed by white policemen in shootouts. Farrakhan cultivates the belief that racism is so deeply entrenched in the white community that blacks are being unfairly hunted and murdered by white policemen.

The concept of fanning the flames of perpetual victimhood and revolution to acquire and sustain power is nothing new. Lenin, Stalin, and Mao well understood the need to keep pushing the us-versus-them mentality to distract populations from the truth and the harsh reality of day-to- day living. Their unscrupulousness paid off.[77]

The one question the revolutionaries never want to address is their end-vision for society, because they don't have one. That is the secret they guard and hide as they manipulate people and foment rage and violence among their followers. Their end goal is not desirable, credible, or useful, but comes down to ultimately advancing their own lust for personal power.[78]

Many among the white segment of the so-called "anti-racism" industry have aided these revolutionary movements, such as the Nation of Islam and Black Lives Matter, by justifying their rage, thereby exposing their own bigotry of low expectations and thus assisting to block the black community from escaping the chains of past slavery and victimhood.

Yet the biggest oppressors of the black community have become their own hate-filled leaders who exploit the community and cause members to keep their eyes focused on the chains of slavery as the community moves through generations of poverty, family breakdown, black-on-black crime and lack of education. They are rendered unable to escape a ghettoized existence.

The oppressed black community has now teamed up with Islamic supremacists and the two are working toward cultivation of goals to indoctrinate and incite revolution against the non-Muslim white society. All the while, peace-loving black and brown people who know and proclaim what these indoctrinators are up to are firmly dismissed as "uncle Toms," "sell-outs," or are ignored. Those who oppose the condescending victimology narrative have also become targets of rage by the profiteers of the anti-racism business, by those indoctrinated by it, and even those who have personally embraced the victim identity.

Farrakhan has called for the murder of police and he did it in the name of "righteousness," "human rights," "justice," and religion as he invoked the Quran. He openly declared:

> "Death is sweeter than to continue to live and bury our children, while white folks give the killer hamburgers.

> "Death is sweeter, than watching us slaughter each other, to the joy of a 400-year-old enemy. Yes, death is sweeter.

> "The Quran teaches persecution is worse than slaughter. Then it says, 'Retaliation is prescribed in matters of the slain.' Retaliation is a prescription from God, to calm the breast of those whose children have been slain.

> "So if the federal government will not intercede in our affairs, then we must rise up and kill those who kill us. Stalk them and kill them and let them feel the pain of death that we are feeling."[79]

There is no systemic stalking of blacks in America or Canada. Farrakhan is a stark example of the power leaders possess to indoctrinate their followers and turn them against authorities of the state, who are there to maintain order and the rule of law. His blatant incitement should have led to his arrest, but the bigotry of low expectations gives him reprieve.

Hatred and incitement to violence and murder against Jews and whites that is deemed to be justified have deep implications for the direction of the West in general. Had a white person proclaimed the violence as Farrakhan did against blacks and Muslims, that person would be punished, and should be.

The Islamic State leader Abu Bakr al-Baghdadi also appealed for white and black men to join hands in unity and so-called "equality" in the name of Allah:

> "It is a state where the Arab and non-Arab, the white man and black man, the easterner and westerner are all brothers," he said—an appeal aimed at broadening his support base beyond the Middle East. "Muslims, rush to your state. Yes, it is your state. Rush, because Syria is not for the Syrians, and Iraq is not for the Iraqis. The earth is Allah's."[80]

There is a problem in the black community stemming from a history of abuse, and this history is now being further abused and exploited by many leaders such as Farrakhan within the black community. Most of them will not brazenly issue an open call to violence and murder as Farrakhan has done, but their silence in the face of such calls, along with the size of Farrakhan's following and influence is revealing.

Another example of the alliance between Black Lives Matter and Islam in the U.S.: in a speech delivered to the Annual Muslim American Society (MAS) and Islamic Circle of North America (ICNA) Convention in December 2015, Nihad Awad, the Executive Director of the Council on American-Islamic Relations (CAIR), urged Muslim Americans to take up the cause of Black Lives Matter. "Black Lives Matter is our matter," he said; "Black Lives Matter is our campaign."[81]

There are clear links between Canada and the United States. Both countries share a continent, therefore, when one sneezes, the other risks catching the cold. To provide some examples: the Black Lives Movement first gained prominence in America before making its way into Canada. Also CAIR, which began in the States, found its way into Canada, as CAIR-CAN and subsequently the NCCM; but in 2018, when President Trump announced his temporary immigration ban on five majority-Muslim countries plus North Korea and Venezuela (Iran, Libya, Somalia, Syria, and Yemen), Prime Minister Trudeau responded by tweeting out an open welcome to refugees. The ramifications are discussed in the Section *"America's National Security Strategy and Why Canada is a Threat: Trudeau, Obama and Trump."*

# 'Anti-Racism' and Opposing Rule of Law

## The Victimology Subterfuge and the Bigotry of Low Expectations

Statistics that the *Washington Post* has been collecting from 2015 to present are revealing:

Police officers killed 732 whites and 381 blacks. The overwhelming majority of those cases involved the officer being attacked, often with a gun. 90 percent of black homicide victims were killed by other black people.[82]

Victimhood is not exclusive to any particular group, but there are malignant influential leaders in the anti-racism industry who are highly divisive and exploitive. Another one of those extreme examples who are tolerated and justified is black Democratic Rep. Maxine Waters, who lives in a neighborhood where houses are valued upward of 2-million-dollars and where her husband collects a pension from the NHL.[83] Waters teamed up with Black Lives Matter protests outside the Capitol in July 2016 in response to two deadly police shootings of black men. It was a protest that disgraced Martin Luther King's peaceful vision of unity in the Civil Rights movement.[84]

The demonstration compared modern day America under black President Barack Obama to the dark days of black oppression that necessitated the civil rights movement. Waters shouted: "I am sick of this s--- and I'm not going to take it anymore."[85] After Waters finished her crowd rousing tirade, the demonstrators chanted as they marched back to the White House: "hands up, don't shoot," "no justice, no peace," and "hey, hey, ho, ho / these racist cops have got to go."[86]

The Black Lives Matter movement is not a peace-loving, pro-black movement as Martin Luther King's movement was before the equalization of blacks under the law. Black Lives Matter is a divisive, violence-promoting movement and a network of well-funded socialist-communist organizations that have been agitating against America for decades.[87]

The Canadian co-founder of Black Lives Matter, Yusra Khogali, tweeted: *"Plz Allah give me strength to not cuss/kill these men and white folks out here today. Plz Plz Plz."* Media outlets who reported on Khogali's words were scrutinized for focusing attention away from other racism issues in the black community.[88]

One needs to seriously review the role of hate-driven revolutionaries that have become regrettably influential in the 'anti-racism' industry.

It should be obvious that Black Lives Matter works contrary to Martin Luther King's ideals, which proclaimed unity and embraced all life. In one of his statements, Martin Luther King strongly condemned violence:

Man was born into barbarism when killing his fellow man was a normal condition of existence. He became endowed with a conscience. And he has now reached the day when violence toward another human being must become as abhorrent as eating another's flesh.[89]

Another example of the alliance between a so-called 'oppressed' group, the Islamic jihad cause, and the socialist left, could be seen when 28-year-old Democratic Socialist Alexandria Ocasio-Cortez, became an instant Democratic Party heroine by unseating party caucus chair Rep. Joe Crowley (D-NY) in the New York primary in June 2018.[90] Ocasio-Cortez is virulently anti-Israel,  and justifies Palestinian terrorism. She accuses Israel of massacring innocent Palestinians during the Gaza demonstrations after Trump moved the American Embassy in Israel to Jerusalem.[91] Israeli forces had in fact shown restraint in carefully targeting jihad terrorists to avoid hitting the many human shields used by HAMAS at the border fence. All the while, HAMAS was setting fire to Israeli fields and launching attacks.  The victims of the massacre that Ocasio-Cortez made a stir about turned out to be 84 percent HAMAS operatives.[92] The rest were human shields, as Israel struggled to defend its border. It is also no surprise that Ocasio-Cortez is against Donald Trump's goal to erect a border fence to keep out illegal aliens crossing over from Mexico.

Lies about victimhood and exploitations of social ills among groups deemed to be oppressed are endemic. Take for example the media explosion that erupted over Trump's so-called family separation policies. Those policies were no different from those of former President Obama.  Trump in fact reversed his and Obama's policy of family separation.

What was not widely known and in fact, largely concealed, was that Trump's approval rating jumped by 10 points among Hispanic voters compared with the month before the controversy.

As reported in a Breitbart article:

"As far as the jump in Hispanic support, that is not at all surprising to those of us who know everyday Hispanics. (My wife is a Mexican immigrant-now-citizen). From my experience, legal immigrants, including Hispanics, resent illegal immigrants even more than everyday Americans do. And why shouldn't they? Legal immigrants followed the rules, went through all the trouble to do things legally. So, naturally, they resent the idea of line jumpers when they waited in line ten years. What's more, illegal aliens take jobs and depress the wages of Hispanic Americans just like they depress the wages of all Americans. While the corrupt media and Democrats want to make illegal immigration about identity politics, according to this poll, Hispanic Americans are not buying it."[93]

No matter what America – or the West—does in terms of correcting its past wrongs such as slavery and colonialism, it will always be deemed collectively "guilty" of racism.

Americans and Westerners have not been able to fathom the hatred against them that is held by the likes of Black Lives Matter, now working with Antifa and the Muslim Brotherhood. Such agenda-driven groups notoriously exploit the victimology narrative, even drawing in innocents to their negative incantations.  As former imam and member of the Muslim Brotherhood front group and unindicted co-conspirator in the 2008 Holy Land Foundation HAMAS terror funding trial, the International Institute for Islamic Thought (IIIT), Abdur-Rahman Muhammad noted:

"Muslims are everywhere in this country, doing practically everything. There are Muslim doctors, lawyers and businessmen—like Park51 developer Sharif El-Gamal, who went from waiting tables just a few years ago to being a multimillionaire. There are Muslim soldiers and CIA agents."[94]

Muhammad went on to say:

"This sense of victimization has now reached a point—especially given the consistent rhetoric of groups like the Council on American-Islamic Relations—that many rank-and-file Muslims now genuinely believe that they are a persecuted and oppressed group."[95]

Now, to return to Maxime Waters. Just after White House press secretary Sarah Sanders was asked to leave a restaurant in Lexington, Virginia, because of her work on President Donald Trump's behalf, Waters publicly incited abuse against the Trump team. She stated:

"Let's make sure we show up wherever we have to show up. And if you see anybody from that Cabinet in a restaurant, in a department store, at a gasoline station, you get out and you create a crowd. And you push back on them. And you tell them they're not welcome anymore, anywhere. We've got to get the children connected to their parents."[96]

In a similar manner but worse, University of California Professor Hatem Bazian, co-founder of the anti-Israel Students for Justice in Palestine, issued an open call for intifada in the United States.[97]

Bazian is not the only American Muslim in a leadership position who has been calling for violent uprising. Arutz Sheva reported on MEMRI's video of Egyptian-born American Imam Ammar Shahin delivering a Friday sermon at the Islamic Center of Davis, northern California, where he called for the slaughter of all Jews.[98]

It is a strange phenomenon that career "anti-racists"—who call themselves human rights activists—are uninterested in the fact that black slavery, sex slavery, systemic racism, sexism, deadly persecution of religious and ethnic minorities are still going on in Islamic states. While these and the Darfur massacres of black Christians are ignored, the long past wrongs of colonialism and American slavery and oppression are being exhumed continuously.

Also, Jews whose families suffered severe abuses in the Holocaust continue to experience ongoing racist attacks and widespread antisemitism today, including attempts to delegitimize and destroy the Jewish homeland of Israel. Despite this, the wealthy Nation of Islam promotes slanderous propaganda against the Jewish people as follows:

> "Jews have been conclusively linked to the greatest criminal endeavor ever undertaken against an entire race of people ... the black African Holocaust. ... The effects of this unspeakable tragedy are still being felt among the peoples of the world at this very hour."[99]

# Today's Anti-Racism Industry — A Divisive Cornerstone

The underlying message conveyed by many leaders of the anti-racism industry today—including some of the CRRF stakeholders that I observed in public forums—is that it is high time that white "colonialist" "oppressors" went to the back of the bus and lived in guilt and shame because of the past sins of their ancestors. For them, descendants of Europeans must embrace permanent shame, to match the permanent victimhood of some visible minorities.

Even POLITICO magazine had to ask the question of the one-time useful Southern Poverty Law Center: has a civil rights stalwart lost its way? In an article, POLITICO stated of the SPLC that "the group has expanded beyond its crusade against racial discrimination in the South, increasingly taking up the left flank of the culture wars on issues like LGBT rights, church-state division, Islam and immigration. The new approach has prompted accusations of overreach."[100] One can now find conservative policy centers like the Family Research Council on the Southern Poverty Law Center's 'hate map,' but not the violent left-wing extremist group antifa."

At the end of July 2018, *Gays Against Sharia* UK announced that it was holding a joint rally with *Standing For Britain*. The group stated on Facebook that the march will protest "against Muslim grooming gangs operating in Stockton." Yet the group's efforts were immediately opposed by anti-fascists who announced a counter protest against the Stockton march. The grounds of antifa was stated in a statement that it is urging "all who oppose racism and Islamophobia" to support its "anti-fascist protest."[101]

The legendary Martin Luther King advocated for equality and human rights for all, a huge contrast to what is tolerated as acceptable in the anti-racism industry today.  In his momentous speech on August 28, 1963 on the steps of the Lincoln Memorial, he shared his vision for unity, cohesion, and harmony between blacks and whites:

> I have a dream that my four little children will one day live in a nation where they will not be judged by the color of their skin but by the content of their character.
>
> I have a *dream* today!
>
> I have a dream that one day, down in Alabama, with its vicious racists, with its governor having his lips dripping with the words of "interposition" and "nullification"—one day right there in Alabama

little black boys and black girls will be able to join hands with little white boys and white girls as sisters and brothers.[102]

Also contrary to this vision, in May 2018, Harvard was met with applause by hosting its first ever graduation for black students only, crowd-funded by students who raised over $27,000.[103]

All-black ceremonies have been held at other American universities, including Stanford and Columbia.[104]

There are those who argue that this does not constitute racism and segregation, that it is different than a graduation for white students only because black people cannot be racist. Only white people can be racist, and only whites can hate and discriminate against blacks because blacks are too oppressed, too wounded, a century and a half later. The low expectation of this perpetually damaged segment of society is insulting and denigrating to the black community and relegates them to a lesser class.

In this model of modern 'anti-racism,' white people will always carry the whip and chains and black people will always be victim.

People tend to forget that America has experienced vast immigration from diverse countries, and also a black president. There is no need today for a black-students-only graduation. It is segregationist.

## America's National Security Strategy and Why Canada Is a Threat: Trudeau, Obama, and Trump

U.S. President Donald J. Trump's National Security Strategy, published in December 2017, flew in the face of every effort by the Organization of Islamic Cooperation (OIC) and those who manipulate the "Islamophobia" subterfuge. It identified the jihad threat to America, a departure from the policy of the Obama administration, which purged any use of language that accurately described the role of Islamic doctrine, law, and scripture in analyzing the ideology behind global Islamic terrorism.

In 2009, a senior Obama White House aide urged the U.S. government to desist from using the term "jihadist"—"asserting that terrorists are simply extremists." Two years later, the White House ordered a scrubbing of all training materials government-wide that Islamic groups deemed to be offensive. The Obama White House then issued a formal edict to remove all teachings on Islam from law enforcement, intelligence, and the military, while the FBI disposed of "pages of information that warned about the threat from the Brotherhood."[105]

In 2013, Army Lt. Col. Matthew Dooley, a decorated officer who taught at the Joint Forces Staff College in Norfolk, Va. was fired by the White House because his course, "'Perspectives on Islam and Islamic Radicals,' discussed how 'political correctness' prevents the military from talking about radical Islam." He wrote that *Political Correctness is killing us: How can we properly identify the enemy, analyze his weaknesses, and defeat him, if we are NEVER permitted to examine him from the most basic doctrinal level?"*[106]

Obama had now provided an open house for Muslim Brotherhood (MB) operatives to work freely in America, emboldening aggressive MB entities. Yet the Muslim Brotherhood Plan for North America is explicit in its objective. "An Explanatory Memorandum: From the Archives of the Muslim Brotherhood in America" was entered as evidence into the largest terrorism funding trial in the history of the United States—the 2008 Holy Land Foundation Trial. The memorandum stated:

> "The process of settlement is a 'Civilization-Jihadist Process' with all the word means. The Ikhwan [Muslim Brotherhood] must understand that their work in America is a kind of grand jihad in eliminating and destroying the Western civilization from within and "sabotaging" its miserable house by their hands and the hands of the believers so that

it is eliminated and God's religion is made victorious over all other religions."[107]

The mission of the Muslim Brotherhood is to impose Islamic law (shariah) worldwide. The "miserable house" referred to in the Memorandum is the House of War (Dar al-Harb), which must be conquered and brought under the House of Islam (Dar al-Islam). Steven Emerson of the Investigative Project on Terrorism, who has long been monitoring the network of Islamic groups with ties to the Muslim Brotherhood, "noted that he had once "given 143 lectures at the FBI, CIA" but was banned under the Obama Administration "from speaking to any U.S. government counterterrorism conferences...Instead, these agencies were ordered to invite Muslim Brotherhood front groups."[108]

The Trudeau government today bears remarkable resemblance to the Obama Administration. It is perhaps even worse, due to Trudeau's reference to the opposition Conservative Party as "Islamophobic" and his dedication to criminalize so-called "Islamophobia" in Canada.

Some other trends in Canada to observe: the Conservative Party sought to defund terrorist-linked groups, strip citizenship from terrorists, implement a zero tolerance policy on "barbaric cultural practices," overwhelmingly voted against the passing of "anti-Islamophobia" Motion M-103 and shut down Iran's embassy in Ottawa. The Liberal Party, conversely, has repealed the Conservative provision to strip the citizenship of terrorists, erased use of the phrase "barbaric cultural practices" and introduced the 'anti-Islamophobia' motion M-103 that referenced the Conservatives as "Islamophobic." Trudeau has defended returning ISIS fighters with a stunning personal passion, while under tough questioning by Conservative opposition leader Andrew Scheer in Parliament.[109]

Upon Trudeau's election win in October 2015, Robert Spencer noted in Frontpage Magazine that Justin Trudeau was Canada's Obama:

The new Prime Minister of Canada, like Obama, has consistently downplayed the nature and magnitude of the jihad threat and ascribed it to other causes. Christine Williams, a Canadian journalist and a Federally appointed Director with the Canadian Race Relations Foundation, has noted that in the wake of the Boston Marathon jihad bombing, Trudeau issued a bizarre statement: "There is no question that this happened because of someone who feels completely excluded, someone who feels completely at war with innocence, at war with society."[110]

Compounding the predicament of Western infiltration by Muslim Brotherhood stealth operatives and threats of both civilizational and violent jihad through unmanaged immigration are Iran's proxies. In 2012, a tight network of Iranian terrorists was discovered to be expanding a "fifth column" in Canada, using its embassy in Ottawa to mobilize loyalists of the Islamic Republic to infiltrate the Canadian government and, some terrorism experts worried, attack the United States. The Iranian embassy was subsequently closed by the Conservatives, marking an end to Canada's diplomatic relations with Iran.[111]

Former Iranian diplomat Abolfazl Eslami says he resigned after 25 years working for the Iranian Foreign Ministry because he could no longer work with the government of Iran. Eslami revealed that Iran had been plotting subversive activities through its embassies in Canada and other countries for years.[112]

This included the regime's collecting of detailed personal and job information of Iranians and Muslim immigrants, including the level of their political and economic influence in the host country, and recording this information in computer software. The most influential people were then hand-picked to infiltrate the Canadian government and influence its image of the Islamic regime, thereby affecting the political decision-making process and affecting policy.[113]

The Iranian regime's proxies run deep. Another important consideration was the established evidence "that the joint enterprise of Iran, Hezbollah and al Qaeda were responsible for the Sept. 11 attacks." Testimony from former senior Iranian intelligence officer-turned defector Abolghasem Mesbahi, was deemed credible by former CIA officers Clare Lopez and Bruce Tefft.[114]

A top Iranian official finally admitted openly for the first time in June 2018 that Iran aided al-Qaeda terrorists, including some of the 9/11 attackers. Iran helped them travel secretly through the Middle East.[115]

Secretary of the Iranian judiciary's High Council for Human Rights and a former diplomat Mohammad-Javad Larijani, said that "their movements [through Iran] were under the complete supervision of the Iranian intelligence," in a recently surfaced interview.[116]

In another notable incident, in April 2013, an al-Qaeda terror plot to derail a New York City-bound passenger train as it crossed the railway over Niagara Falls was thwarted by the Royal Canadian Mounted Police. "Perhaps the biggest surprise to come out of the announcement is that the orders were given by al-Qaeda leaders in Iran."[117]

Despite these facts, the Canadian Liberal government has sought to reopen Canada's Iranian embassy and restore relations with Iran. Canadian emissaries made two trips to Tehran as Trudeau's government inched "closer to re-establishing diplomatic ties with Iran."[118]

Iranian Canadian Member of Parliament Majid Jowhari lobbied the Canadian government for this purpose. In fact, Jowhari went so far as to sponsor a petition in 2016 with over 5,600 names, to re-establish diplomatic ties with Iran.[119]

Then, out of the blue, in mid-June 2018—less than two weeks after Foreign Affairs Minister Chrystia Freeland stated that "Canada is not contemplating ending talks with Iran"— the Trudeau government backed a Conservative motion in the House of Commons denouncing Iran, which, in effect, ended the Liberal goal of normalizing relations with Iran. Conservative Opposition Leader Andrew Scheer tweeted out:

> After months pursuing a wrongheaded policy appeasing Iran, Liberals finally agreed with our @CPC_HQ position. But moments after last night's vote, Justin Trudeau's officials signaled they would ignore the will of Parliament. Today, Trudeau refused to provide a straight answer.[120]

Only days before Trudeau's sudden turn on Iran, his Liberal government voted to weaken Canada's anti-terrorism laws, at a time when dozens of known Islamic State jihadists returned to Canada  and while every major Canadian city has operational jihadist terrorist cells.  The Liberal government passed a bill to limit the powers of security agencies in disrupting active terror plots. The bill added more red tape and roadblocks to time-sensitive investigations that could potentially halt an attack in progress.[121]

Now that the Trump Administration is in power in America, the counter-jihad discourse has changed dramatically. The word "jihad" has returned to the table, as is fitting in order to understand the nature of global Islamic terrorism. Most revealing was the contrast between the Trump administration and those of the Obama and Trudeau administrations when Trump revealed his National Security Strategy (NSS) in December 2017. Pillar I of the NSS was to "Protect the American People, the Homeland, and the American Way of Life," by "strengthening control over our borders and immigration system [which is] is central to national security, economic prosperity, and the rule of law."[122]

The National Security Strategy includes important information that illustrates a deep understanding of the jihad threat—domestically and abroad—and of America's core values and principles of democracy. This is completely in contrast to the stance of the Trudeau government. Included in the Strategy:

1. "Jihadist terrorist organizations present the most dangerous terrorist threat to the Nation. America, alongside our allies and partners, is fighting a long war against these fanatics who advance a totalitarian vision for a global Islamist caliphate that justifies murder and slavery, promotes repression, and seeks to undermine the American way of life. Jihadist terrorists use virtual and physical networks around the world to radicalize isolated individuals, exploit vulnerable populations, and inspire and direct plots."[123]

2. "America's core principles, enshrined in the Declaration of Independence, are secured by the Bill of Rights, which proclaims our respect for fundamental individual liberties beginning with the freedoms of religion, speech, the press, and assembly. Liberty, free enterprise, equal justice under the law, and the dignity of every human life are central to who we are as a people. These principles form the foundation of our most enduring alliances, and the United States will continue to champion them. Governments that respect the rights of their citizens remain the best vehicle for prosperity, human happiness, and peace. In contrast, governments that routinely abuse the rights of their citizens do not play constructive roles in the world."[124]

3. "We are under no obligation to offer the benefits of our free and prosperous community to repressive regimes and human rights abusers. We may use diplomacy, sanctions, and other tools to isolate states and leaders who threaten our interests and whose actions run contrary to our values. We will not remain silent in the face of evil. We will hold perpetrators of genocide and mass atrocities accountable."[125]

Trump also included his commitment to "Preserve Peace Through Strength," and crucially important was the recognition that "we learned the difficult lesson that when America does not lead, malign actors fill the void to the disadvantage of the United States.[126] "

The state of Canada now is such that "malign actors" have increased in strength, while "core principles" and values of democratic rights and freedoms are diminishing with the calculated erosion of free speech.

Following Trump's Executive Order to temporarily ban travelers from seven countries of concern, mostly Muslim, Trudeau immediately tweeted out a welcome to refugees: "To those fleeing persecution, terror & war, Canadians will welcome you, regardless of your faith. Diversity is our strength #WelcomeToCanada."[127]

The top five countries of origin for refugee arrivals to Canada in 2016 were: Syria: 33,266, Eritrea: 3,934, Iraq: 1,650, Congo: 1,644, Afghanistan: 1,354, with plans for more.[128]

Despite Trump's responsible and vigilant efforts to combat the jihadist threat both stealthy and violent, America shares a porous border with Canada, which poses a potential threat to the national security of the United States, given the length and breadth of the Islamic supremacist influence in Canada. The U.S.-Canadian border is approximately 3,987 miles long. Add to that the Alaska-Canada border at 1,538 miles. By way of comparison, the U.S.-Mexican border is roughly 1,933 miles.[129]

# CONCLUSION

There is undoubtedly racism, intolerance, and discrimination among white people in white majority countries, but there is also racism and intolerance among visible minorities which is not addressed in the anti-racism industry. Words like "multiculturalism," "diversity," "tolerance," and "inclusion" are benign in and of themselves, but they have been misused, politicized, and taken out of context. Multiculturalism has come to mean that all cultures are equal no matter how abusive some practices acceptable within those cultures might be. Diversity has come to be invoked to force Western populations to accept abuses by foreign cultures; for example, Muslim Member of UK Parliament Naz Shah retweeted that the victims of Muslim rape gangs should "shut up for the good of diversity."[130] Tolerance has also been promoted to mean acceptance of the intolerable, such as barbaric acts committed in the name of Islam, while "inclusion" means that to call out human rights abuses is to be labelled as non-inclusive, "Islamophobic," "racist," etc.

Canada is well-known for its Multicultural Act, being the first country in the world to officially adopt it. Under the Act, it is recognized that "every individual is equal before and under the law" and that "all Canadians, whether by birth or by choice, enjoy equal status, are entitled to the same rights, powers, and privileges and are subject to the same obligations, duties, and liabilities."[131] Critics of multiculturalism have valid concerns that Canada's multicultural edicts are too liberally applied, allowing immigrants to enter Canada, claim full equality of culture and are protected in their continuance of barbaric cultural practices (such as polygamy, subjugation of women, and female genital mutilation etc.). If such practices are condemned, as they should be, as un-Canadian, it is deemed to be "racist." Canada's broad application of multiculturalism was not intended to function this way.

I was fired for writing for Jihad Watch, a site which exposes the truth about Islamic doctrine, law, and scriptures and about the highly organized networks—stealthy and violent—which operate globally and in tandem in order to subvert democracies. Such facts are based on Islamic scriptures, long-established doctrine, published works, and the authorities of Islam, both historical and current.

What is most confusing and unbelievable to the average Westerner is the notion of civilizational jihad, which is documented by the Muslim

Brotherhood. It is a highly sophisticated process as revealed in the Brotherhood's Explanatory Memorandum, in which infiltration and subversion are key.

Despite such irrefutable evidence, a denial persists to the peril of Western civilization. This denial is aided by many mainstream human rights groups. Whether that denial is witting or unwitting is not the important issue, as the outcome of aiding the stealth jihad is the same. There is no time for ignorance during the global jihad wars. Take for example, the Anti-Defamation League, which states this about the founder of the Center of Security Policy, Frank Gaffney:

> Gaffney has promulgated a number of anti-Muslim conspiracy theories over the years. Chief among them is the allegation that the U.S. government has been infiltrated by the Muslim Brotherhood and that a number of political figures have actual ties to the group.[132]

Gaffney has elucidated traceable, well-documented facts, yet stealth jihadists know all too well that Westerners lack knowledge about Muslim Brotherhood goals and Islamic doctrine. Under shariah, it is apostasy to criticize Islam, Muhammad, to challenge the ulema, Islamic doctrine, as well as stymie the obligation to expand as set forth in Islamic doctrine and law. Even the 'mainstream' *New York Times* published the Explanatory Memorandum by the Muslim Brotherhood on February 9, 2017, but despite this, Gaffney and others who warn about the dangers of Islamization are branded "Islamophobic," "racist," "anti-diversity," "white supremacist," and the like. Even the Somali-born Ayaan Hirsi Ali was branded a "white supremacist" by a group of Australian Muslim women who opposed her speaking in Australia. Hirsi Ali, whose trip was subsequently cancelled, replied that these Muslim women were "apologists for terror groups."[133]

Stealth jihadists are well-versed in manipulating the Western promotion of diversity and multiculturalism in their continued struggle to subjugate the House of War. To accomplish this, the Muslim Brotherhood, its associates and a contingent of other Islamic apologists have been on a mission to distance themselves from association with violent jihadists, so as to not frighten Westerners. This scheme clears the path for them successfully to creep in to advance their agenda in Europe, U.S., and Canada, in the latter of which Trudeau's Liberal Government has an Islamic supremacist entryist problem, as discussed earlier.

The anti-racism industry, with its mandate to promote a damaging version of multiculturalism, diversity, and tolerance, has now been swindled by stealth Islamic supremacist operatives into providing a banner under which they can claim victimhood and manipulate an agenda. In Canada, the Government has outlined an action plan to crack down on "Islamophobia," working hand in hand with Muslim Brotherhood-linked organizations like the NCCM and IRFAN and providing funding for their efforts.

The book "Jihad is the Way" was written by Mustafa Mashhur, the official leader of the Muslim Brotherhood in Egypt from 1996-2002. The book is the fifth volume of a complete work called *The Laws of Da'wa* (Islamic missionary activity) and was translated by Palestinian Media Watch. In it, Mashhur explains in full detail the Muslim Brotherhood's beliefs and aspirations.[134] Critical is the role of violent Jihad in bringing about a world under Islam, *i.e.*, subjugating the House of War to the House of Islam. Mashhur's teachings encompass subjects such as the Islamic duty to establish an Islamic state, world domination under Islam, the public and personal religious duty of military Jihad, in full use of the power of arms and weapons.

Included in the book:

- "Jihad is a religious public duty... incumbent upon the Islamic nation. Jihad is a personal duty to fend off the infidels' attack on the nation ..."

- "The youth should know that the problems of the Islamic world, such as Palestine, Afghanistan, Syria, Eritrea, or the Philippines, are not issues of territories and nations, but of faith and religion. They are problems of Islam and the Muslims, and they can be resolved neither by negotiation nor by recognizing the enemy's right to the Islamic land he stole. Rather, the only option is Jihad for Allah, and this is why Jihad is the way."

- "The symbol of the [Muslim] Brotherhood is the book of Allah [the Quran] between two swords. The swords symbolize Jihad and the force that protects the truth represented in Allah's book."

- "You should be prepared to answer the call of Jihad whenever you are called, in any region of the Islamic world. Our Islam is universal not regional, and all Islamic countries are one homeland. Timing: Don't rush, prepare carefully for Jihad.[135]

One can easily observe the overlap between violent and stealth jihad when 9-11 leader Khalid Sheik Mohammed stated:

"We will win because Americans don't realize....we do not need to defeat you militarily; we only need to fight long enough for you to defeat yourself by quitting....large-scale attacks such as 9/11 were nice, but not necessary...jihadi-minded brothers would immigrate into the United States...wrap themselves in America's rights and laws," until they were strong enough to rise up and attack. He also stated that the "American people would eventually become so tired, so frightened, and so weary of war that they would just want it to end."[136]

Like the fox guarding the henhouse, Muslim Brotherhood operatives have deeply infiltrated public and private sectors of Western societies, under the banner of the anti-racism industry, and are "teaching" leaders and citizens alike about the "benign" and peaceful nature of Islam, and the need to "quell" "Islamophobia," which includes a climate of hate, fear, and dislike of Islam. This infiltration is abundantly evident in the Canadian Heritage Department follow-up to M-103, "Taking Action Against Systemic Racism and Religious Discrimination Including Islamophobia," as described earlier.

My firing from the Canadian Race Relations Foundation was inevitable given the path that was followed by the Heritage Department and the role that the CRRF had found itself under in Melanie Joly's Department of Heritage.

## The West Has Evolved While the Anti-Racism Industry Clings to the Past

Europe and the Americas have dramatically changed in demographic composition. Due to the historic, celebrated and much-needed efforts of genuine anti-racism and discrimination activists, we owe much to those who fought to dismantle the chains and barriers that once prevented the evolution and development of a multi-racial society.

Diverse populations can now be seen in all spheres of Western life: the corporate boardroom, politics, in science, medicine, the arts, education, entertainment, and sports, etc. It took collaborative, strenuous efforts to achieve such a mosaic and this endeavor should continue to advance. It is imperative that this evolution continue.

The biggest challenge facing the West today is managing immigration. The first step is to recognize, accept, and admit to a profound truth that is so far being avoided: all cultures are not equal, but all people are equal in human dignity and under the law.

Advanced and evolved Western societies that enshrine gender equality and equality among races and creeds are societies that provide a safety-net from oppressive societies which do not recognize such rights or at least, they should provide such a safety-net. They cannot do so, however, if they 'tolerate' the intolerable into their multicultural societies in the name of 'diversity,' Christian persecution, sex slavery, black slavery, child marriage, penalties for criticism of an ideology, stonings, beheadings, a family murdering a young female family member for bringing shame to the family, etc., are severely abusive and should not be condoned or accommodated in Western societies.

To recognize these abuses does not presume that Western countries are free from racism, abuses, sex attacks, murders, domestic abuses, etc. One strategy of Muslim Brotherhood affiliates is to point out that Western societies also have abuse of females. In Western countries, though, such abuses are illegal, penalized, frowned upon, and unacceptable as they should be, whereas under Islamic Law, they are doctrinally permitted or even obligatory. Women are legal equals in Western societies despite the various human defects.

The West has constructed laws which serve to protect all citizens without partiality. There are no excuses for abuses and none should be accepted. If anyone abuses or discriminates in the name of a belief system, this must be recognized, discussed, and rejected. Truth and freedoms must transcend wounded feelings, particularly when sheltering wounded feelings enables the continuance of abuses. Until Muslims learn to take criticisms as do adherents of every other belief system, they cannot be considered modernized, tolerant, and pluralistic. They have a citizenship responsibility in a two-way street relationship in democratic societies and must face consequences for violations of Western laws and mores. They are not special by way of their belief system, nor are they superior but are equals. We are engaged in a jihad war against the West and it is important that Western leaders awaken from their sleep, learn about other cultures, religions—and how they differ from Western democracies— set boundaries and live by them as responsible leaders should for the sake of unity, true diversity, pluralism, and in protecting homeland security.

Once upon a time, blacks were held as slaves by whites, there was also white oppression of blacks, colonialism, barriers to jobs due to race, but those days are long gone. Racism still exists, as well as sexism, but so do human prejudices based on a person's appearance, height, weight, social competence, mental acuity, and so on. In addition, there is inter-immigrant intolerance and racism, and also virulent hatred of white people that exists among visible minority groups—some based on historic wrongs and some based strictly on supremacist ideas.

Part of the solution is to move forward in the confident application of the democratic rule of law. This begins with the complete rejection of: human rights abuses from any culture, the excuses made to perpetuate such abuses, and foreign networks that seek to harm another race of people or those of another creed. We must also try to keep foreign wars and their battles from entering Western countries.

If the West chooses to welcome immigrants, immigrants must conform to Western freedoms and the rule of law. Democracies are fully actualized as bastions of human rights and the only way forward is to perfect their implementation, however much work there remains to do. It is impossible to have any human society that is completely free of prejudices, but it is worth progressive efforts.

## An Urgent Need to Take Back Democracy and Human Rights

It is not complicated for Western leaders to reject all forms of Islamic supremacist blasphemy laws, and to reject Islamic Law (shariah), which has no place in democratic institutions. Islamic States are governed by shariah and it is a stratagem of conquest to convince democratic leaders that shariah is compatible with free, democratic societies-when even the most cursory of contrasts will demonstrate that it is not. Democratic institutions are not in need of shariah state advice. Any verbose lobby groups trying to explain why their group needs special attention should raise red flags.

There are substantial numbers of Western visible minority immigrants who are appalled by the manipulation of democracy and the immigration system by social justice warriors, angry revolutionaries and Islamic supremacists. Under these established systems, peaceful immigrants had to wait their turn in line, navigate through culture shock and earn their respect (first through self-respect), oftentimes in the midst of poverty, language barriers, discrimination, and more.

Equally appalling are white leftists who claim to know more about foreign cultures and races than those from those same foreign cultures and races they profess to defend. These leftists are quick to brand conservative white people as racists, when they are the worst racists themselves because they ascribe to the (previously explained) bigotry of low expectations and are extraordinarily arrogant in spite of their flagrant ignorance. They oddly instead ally themselves with angry, supremacist visible minority leaders who manipulate them, use them, and exploit their ignorance.

**Real Dialogue and Pluralism Must Be Restored**

Conversation and dialogue cannot and must not be restricted. If it is deemed to be hate to call out behaviors of a race, creed or ideology that is concerning, then more discussion is needed, not less. It was not racism to call out Nazism because not all Germans were Nazis. It was not racism to call out Soviet Communism because not all people from the Soviet Union were communists. It is not racism to criticize the policies of North Korea because not all North Koreans are oppressively dictatorial. It is not racism to call out communist China because all Chinese people are not Communists. Under the authority of each of those regimes, however, open criticism was and is forbidden according to their oppressive doctrines. Finally, it is not racism or "Islamophobic" to call out Islamic doctrine as specified in the authoritative Islamic texts when speaking under the shelter of democratic constitutions.

The anti-racism industry has been overshadowed by the "anti-Islamophobia" victimology narrative, which is propagandist, unforgiving, self-indulgent, and divisive. The perpetration of the "Islamophobia" narrative in a multicultural country, with the added malady of wide-open borders, is a ruinous development for democracy and the rule of law.

To advance a united West under a banner of pluralism, human rights, and democracy requires that the supremacist root of special privilege end. No belief system, doctrine or ideology coming into Western countries should be immune from scrutiny, and any ideology that sanctions the treatment of another human being as inferior must be rejected. To be above scrutiny is to be above liberal Western democratic constitutions and once a force becomes so powerful, it is now a supremacist force and any group or idea beneath it becomes the inferior entity.

Shariah holds that Islam is superior, and therefore must not be criticized or scrutinized and that Muhammad must not be insulted. These doctrines and ideas have no place in a democracy and should be firmly rejected along with any shariah doctrine that does not align with democratic principles. No human is deemed to have more value than another in a democracy. The loaded word "Islamophobia" must be replaced with "anti-Muslim bigotry" if Western nations are to further advance as bastions of human rights for all.

When an us-versus-them mentality is fostered, so is conflict, which inevitably fans the flames of the worst supremacist elements in the darkest corners of society.

Some of these dark corners unfortunately have included mosques, and I landed in hot water for suggesting that it was time to surveil mosques. Yet in 2011, Israeli terrorism expert and researcher Mordechai Kedar, along with his American counterpart David Yerushalmi, undertook an extensive survey of mosques in the U.S., and concluded:

> "Unfortunately, the results of the current survey strongly suggest that Islam—as it is generally practiced in mosques across the United States—continues to manifest a resistance to the kind of tolerant religious and legal framework that would allow its followers to make a sincere affirmation of liberal citizenship. This survey provides empirical support for the view that mosques across America, as institutional and social settings for mosque-going Muslims, are at least resistant to social cooperation with non-Muslims. Indeed, the overwhelming majority of mosques surveyed promoted literature supportive of violent jihad and a significant number invited speakers known to have promoted violent jihad and other behaviors that are inconsistent with a reasonable construct of liberal citizenship."[137]

Dr. Sheikh Subhy Mansour, founder of the Quranist sect in Egypt, states:

> "I stood against the Saudi influence and suffered. ... When I came here to the US, I had dreams and ideas, because this was America. But when I went to mosque, I found the same people, advocating the same Shariah. I escaped from there and found them here, so I said to myself, what could I do after that? Escape to the Moon?" With regard to Muslim Brotherhood organizations on American soil, he warns that they "exploit the American values of freedom of expression and freedom of religion to brainwash American Muslims to prevent their integration into the American society. They even try to turn them into enemies of their country and their fellow citizens....Salafists are like untamed animals, saying what's in their hearts, but the Muslim Brotherhood is very cunning, intelligent, and they know what to say and what to conceal, but they have the same ideas of the Salafis, but the latter is very primitive. They say publicly what is in their heart.[138]

Dr. Tawfik Hamid was once drawn into the Muslim Brotherhood circle around Ayman al-Zawahiri—the current Al-Qa'eda leader. He is a medical doctor and formerly Senior Fellow and Chair for the Study of Islamic Radicalism at the Potomac Institute for Policy Studies. He states:

> "At the high levels of the Muslim Brotherhood, the desire is to dominate the world, and when you are close with them as I was, you will feel it in their words. They will not come and say it in your face in the West, but they certainly do it in their private talks. They say that they see decay

in the Western civilization and an ultimate collapse, that failure is going to happen, and they see themselves as the ones who will provide the replacement for it."[139]

Shariah-adherent mosques are not exclusive to any one location, as "Saudi Arabia's export of the rigid, bigoted, patriarchal, fundamentalist" Wahhabism has fueled global jihad, both stealth and violent. This great Revivalist Movement of the eighteenth century, founded by Abd Al-Wahhab, was intended to return Islam back to its earliest authentic form, deemed to be the purest form of Islam because it was the Islam of Muhammad and his earliest followers, the Salafis. Meanwhile, on the Shi'ite side of things, Iran's Islamic Revolutionary Guard Corps, created by the late Ayatollah Khomeini, was created to secure the revolution at home and then to export it abroad.[140] Now, news has emerged that Turkish President Recep Tayyip Erdogan's re-election was fueling valid concerns about his growing powers not just in his own country but in America, where experts have exposed Erdogan's determination to spread his Islamic "nationalistic fervor through a network of mosques and religious centers."[141]

While in Iceland, I was informed that the Islamic Cultural Center in Iceland was Saudi-funded. It later emerged that its Imam Ahmad Sedeeq, who was present at a lecture Robert Spencer and I gave in Reykjavik on May 11, 2017, stated that the London Bridge jihadi massacre, in which 8 people were killed and 48 injured, was staged, and actors were made to play the victims.[142]

Sedeeq attempted to obstruct my talk several times, in an attempt to refute facts about stonings in shariah-adherent countries. I also later came across an article in Iceland Magazine dated November 24, 2015: *"President of Iceland fears Saudi Arabian funding of Reykjavík Mosque will fuel Muslim extremism in Iceland."* Recall that it was *"My Warning to Icelanders"* that contributed to the Government of Canada expelling me for warning about Islamic supremacist deceptions. Even Israel's ambassador to Germany, Yakov Hadas-Handelsman, points out that "the time has come for the Germans and the Europeans to understand what is hidden behind the Iranian smile" as he referenced Iranian proxies who were spying on the Israeli embassy and the Jewish community, including schools.

My termination from the CRRF had ramifications in Iceland; I received an email from a main organizer of the event in Reykjavik featuring Robert Spencer and me. I was notified via email by a Vakur leader that:

"A DV article was shared widely on Facebook which eventually resulted in a spokesman of the Pirate party (which has six Members of

Parliament) separating himself (in a comment on Facebook) from Bjartmar (he is a member of the Pirate party and has been far down on their list of candidates). He said that these actions of Bjartmar had nothing to do with the party, that Bjartmar was acting on his own, and his behavior did not reflect in any way the Pirates' point of view."

It remains curious that Joly would accuse me of violating the CRRF mandate of promoting diversity, inclusion, and respect for democracy, when this is precisely what I did (and continue to do) routinely in my writings outside of my CRRF work. In writing for Jihad Watch, I am confronted daily by the assaults upon the dignity of humankind by jihadists and Islamic supremacists, who invoke their religious texts to justify their actions, as well as to advance their expansionist shariah agenda onto Western soil.

History has taught that oppressive, human rights-violating regimes never allow free speech, and they inevitably seize control of the media. The media becomes the mouthpiece of the supremacist leadership. This is the state of affairs building in multicultural Canada and in other once-democratic states that are now in decline.

Far too many of Canada's political class yield to activists who manipulate multiculturalism to attract the immigrant vote. Even before he was elected, Liberal Prime Minister Justin Trudeau gave a speech at the Reviving the Islamic Spirit conference in Toronto, whose foremost sponsor was IRFAN-Canada (International Relief Fund for the Afflicted and Needy). It was discussed earlier that IRFAN was stripped of its federal charity status for supporting HAMAS.[143]

CAIR condemned attempts to "smear" the gathering, while CAIR-CAN/NCCM came out in defense of the convention, labeling criticism of IRFAN-Canada's sponsorship of the event as "yet another example of Islamophobic vitriol aimed at marginalizing and vilifying Muslims."[144]

**The Anti-Racism Industry Manipulated to Serve the Civilizational Jihad**

Canada's multicultural experiment has become a left-wing/right- wing point of divide, which prevents the implementation of effective policies to combat the manipulation of the multiculturalist ethos by Islamic lobbies which are well-attuned to the powers of the multicultural voting bloc and encourage outreach by politicians to their communities. Competing rights and interests exist in America, even in the absence of a multicultural act, so to focus on blaming the Act, which is likely here to stay, is to divert necessary attention away from confronting Muslim Brotherhood, and other Islamic Movement exploitations, and creating policies to stem them. The circular debate on the merits and flaws of Canada's commitment to multiculturalism prevents rational discussion of policies to contain Muslim Brotherhood/Islamic supremacist infiltration.

Potent prescriptions to this malady are free speech, open and honest dialogue, and the marginalizing of individuals who employ racism and identity politics for personal greed. These individuals are recognized by their bigotry of low expectations, their alliances with unindicted co-conspirators to jihad terrorism, their advancing of the us-versus-them game, their sustained branding and marketing of the "white privilege" narrative, and their blindness to the successes of blacks and Muslims in mainstream society.

These types of individuals cluster in the diversity and anti-racism industry and they will not hear of it that intolerance, racism, and bigotry of the worst kind are doctrinal in mainstream Islam. They will also not hear of it that Western societies are importing barbaric shariah practices like Female Genital Mutilation (FGM) through uncontrolled immigration and refugee policies which is bringing continued harm to women and girls. Many of these women and girls who left their home countries rightly expect to escape barbaric practices like FGM and now instead, these practices are being imported, bringing harm also to the host societies.

Faux human rights and anti-racism advocates have become modern-day enablers of oppression and traitors to democratic freedoms. They aid the very demons they profess to oppose: supremacism, privilege, intolerance, and oppression, as embodied in Islamic doctrine, law, and scripture. They also stir division and tensions through identity politics and shut down dialogue and pluralism.

Integration is a crucial challenge facing Western societies today, of which a fundamental point needs to be grasped by leaders: that democratic doctrines of human rights and freedoms are superior to doctrines of Islamic Law (or shariah) societies. This is not to say that any human beings are inferior. Many leaders struggle to grasp the difference between a human being and a doctrine. To such leaders, rightly requiring immigrants to leave all barbaric and liberty-destroying doctrines at the door is insulting and essentially the same as telling that person that they are unwelcome. Western leaders have failed to set boundaries.

As a rule, if a person or group cannot accept the rules of the democratic nation that he or she is emigrating to, then such a person should not live in a democracy. If his or her intention is to subvert the democracy, then it becomes the responsibility of democratic leaders to be guardians of their constitution and protect the citizenry, and homeland security.

With respect to the difficulties within the black community, blacks—like every oppressed group throughout history—must be accepted as equals to every other race, and they must also see themselves as equals, not as perpetual victims. This holds true for anyone who may have been victimized.

Victimology has become a justifiable reason to break the law, incite violence, stir anarchy and bring harm innocents, as we see promoted within the Nation of Islam and Black Lives Matter. A related phenomenon to victimhood is hastening to attribute jihad to "mental illness." Such misuse of a genuine medical diagnosis demeans the medical profession as well as those who unfortunately suffer from the actual condition. On a clear Sunday night on July 22, 2018, a Muslim man, 29-year-old Faisal Hussain, calmly walked down Danforth Avenue in Toronto's Greektown, a popular area known for its restaurants and cafes. He pulled out a gun and sprayed innocents with bullets. He murdered a 10-year-old girl and an 18-year-old woman, before turning the gun on himself.[145]

Right after the Ontario Special Investigations Unit revealed Hussain's identity, a carefully crafted news release was sent out to select media by the "Hussain Family." It began with the family's expression of "deepest condolences to the families who are now suffering on account of our son's horrific actions" and explained that "our son had severe mental health challenges, struggling with psychosis and depression his entire life." As it turns out, the "Hussain Family" statement was provided by "spin doctor" Mohammed Hashim, "described as a driving force behind the National Council of Canadian Muslims."[146]

A bio of Hashim touts "his groundbreaking political advocacy, public relations and media work has been widely credited by insiders as framing a new narrative for Muslims in Canada." His bio continued: "His workshop 'Progressive organizing in the Muslim communities' will demonstrate how the GTA Muslim community mobilized in the previous federal election and laid the groundwork to start building a national political movement."[147]

The usual "anti-racism," diversity-promoting players bit the bait. In article after article, readers endured being lectured to about Hussain's mental illness and the problem with guns, even though Canada has strict gun controls and Hussain's gun was illegally acquired. One of the voices was Bernie Farber, who wrote in a joint commentary for the Toronto Star after my firing from the CRRF, that "Christine Douglass-Williams, a board member of the Canadian Race Relations Foundation, was ousted for Islamophobic commentary."[148]

Upon release of the "Hussain Family" clever letter, Farber rushed to the defense of Hussain. He declared that *This was not terrorism. This was not hatred. This was not extremism. It was a sad and disturbed life, a man whose mind turned against him and led him to commit an unspeakable act of depravity."*[149]

Farber is the executive director of the far-left Mosaic Institute in Toronto. I could never forget a public lecture during a CRRF symposium, when a Mosaic Institute representative and speaker stated that there is no such thing as imported conflict, only imported trauma. It is a feature narrative of the Mosaic Institute.[150] Farber also once served as a panelist in a community event organized as part of the Mosaic Institute's "In Conversation Series." The event was called "Canada in a Trump World," which also featured National Council of Canadian Muslims Executive Director Ihsaan Gardee.[151] The Mosaic Institute has a longtime relationship with the NCCM and endorsed its "Charter for Inclusive Communities."[152]

Despite Farber's instant conclusion, Hussain's neighbors knew nothing of his "mental illness."[153] A police source stated about Hussain: "He had seven magazines with him and each magazine carries between 12 and 15 bullets.... It could have easily been 100 bullets or more."[154] One officer said in his years on the job, he has never come across a shooter better with a gun than Hussain. The officer went on "He was very proficient," said the officer. "I can't imagine he could change magazines on the run, avoid jamming and hit targets as accurately as he did, had he not had some firearms training and experience."[155] Hussain was also known to police and had expressed support for a pro-Islamic State website.[156]

Those who wish to engage in anti-racism initiatives should be promoting democratic values and the need for immigrants to integrate. They should be particularly knowledgeable about immigrant groups as a prerequisite, both the good and also the problematic issues that affect groups. The industry today has not progressed beyond "white colonialism," "white racism," and black slavery as a result of white slave-owners. They either know nothing—or are willfully blind—about: inter-group racism, intolerance and discrimination among various immigrant groups, Islamic jurisprudence, Islamic supremacism, racism, and black slavery within the Islamic world, and a host of abuses already highlighted in this work. Most do not even know that the Arabic word "*abd*," (in some uses akin to the n-word, but literally meaning both "black" and "slave"), is still used by Arabs without condemnation. Their woeful lack of knowledge renders them completely ill-equipped as they advocate for open borders while knowing nothing about who is entering those borders and what some of their agendas may be.

Anti-racism individuals working within the black community should be teaching about the merits of education, and hard work and noting that the doors of opportunity are open, and also that the values of a stable family and of working harmoniously within and outside of their community are prized values. Blacks undeniably have been victimized, but they also need to let go of victimhood as a group identity, and to realize that there are many modern-day group victims who have shed their victimhood to become fully integrated, productive and active members of mainstream society—for instance, Jews who survived the Holocaust, Chinese whose families were massacred and oppressed by the Japanese, Japanese who were oppressed in internment camps, Indians who were abused as indentured laborers etc. These groups have collectively learned to thrive well in Western societies through self-acceptance, education and hard work. They did not embrace perpetual rage and bitterness as a group identity as Western societies evolved; nor did they have leaders among their own races fueling such a negative group identity.

Modern revolutionaries, such as the Muslim Brotherhood, Black Lives Matter, and jihadist indoctrinators—who stoke rage, violence, and uprising in Western societies that have long evolved, need to be confronted and resisted, as they aggressively enable and exploit victimhood. Left unattended to, societal discord will continue to gain momentum; and the rule of law will be weakened. Socialist-left enablers are being utilized by modern revolutionary groups, socialists and other leftists are also using these groups to serve their own personal ambitions; and so the alliance endures and grows.

It obviously advances the socialist-left and jihadist alliance to exploit the anti-racism industry for political gain. The anti-racism industry instead needs to evolve into one that subscribes to the principles of equal rights for all.

Some of the quotes that emerged in the Toronto Star after my termination:

1. "A [Liberal] government source told the Star she was removed because of comments she has made online which 'do not reflect the goal of the foundation.' "[157]

2.  "'Jihad Watch is one of the leading voices pushing Islamophobic sentiment today,' Amarnath Amarasingam, a prominent Canadian researcher of terrorism and Islam, said in an email. 'The idea that someone who sits on the Canadian Race Relations Foundation's board would have anything to do with Jihad Watch or Robert Spencer is mind-boggling to me.' "[158]

3.  "The National Council of Canadian Muslims also expressed concerns and sent a formal letter to the government in October. Executive director Ihsaan Gardee said Douglass-Williams' removal is an 'appropriate corrective measure taken by government to address (her) disturbing public record. The removal of Ms. Douglass-Williams is long overdue in light of her known Islamophobic commentary and her public association with purveyors of hateful propaganda, such as Robert Spencer who has long been identified by human rights institutions as a leading figure of the Islamophobia movement in North America.'"[159]

4.  "Heidi Beirich, director of the Southern Poverty Law Center's Intelligence Project, said Douglass-Williams has been 'on the anti-Muslim circuit for some time and has written hundreds of articles for Jihad Watch since 2012."[160]

Islamic supremacism is a global threat, and its doctrine has spread deeply into the West. Its purveyors are those linked to the Muslim Brotherhood and other Islamic Movement groups including violent jihad groups like al-Qa'eda and the Islamic State. The Holy Land Foundation trial, mentioned earlier, revealed the dominant role of HAMAS—the Palestinian branch of the Muslim Brotherhood. In the words of Israel's ambassador to the UN, Danny Danon: "[T]he time has come for the Security Council to recognize that HAMAS is no different from al-Qaeda or ISIS."[161] The goal is expansion and conquest of the House of War even though the apparent strategies might differ. One must also remember that the Muslim Brotherhood also espouses violent jihad, so that the more emboldened it becomes, the more violent it will become as is noted in Egypt; *i.e.*, until they achieve complete rulership.

The Muslim Brotherhood in the West is now so advanced and its networks so deeply intertwined in the anti-racism industry that a match made in hell has developed: The Islamic Movement has cultivated an alliance with revolutionary victimology groups like Black Lives Matter, the very wealthy Nation of Islam, and also drug cartels. Even depression and mental health problems among young Muslims can now be harnessed and cultivated by unscrupulous jihadist leaders into revolution as jihad is the highest calling. What is deemed to be a psychopathology in Western society has been shaped and molded into goals toward so-called 'martyrdom' in the Islamic Movement project.

Civilizational jihad is advancing toward the conquest of the House of War amid the scarcity of education about the tactics of the Islamic Movement, especially the Muslim Brotherhood. All organizations on Western soil which have known links to foreign jihadi groups should be held accountable for the preservation of freedoms, equal rights and the rule of law. The goal of such groups is subversion and Western democracies have no organized strategies in place for how to contend with these stealth jihadist groups, which have seized leadership roles among us. They operate on taxpayer dollars in every sphere of Western life and have been influencing everything from school curricula to election campaigns.

It was once impossible to envision that Canada would become a country in which punitive measures would be levied against those who criticized the advance of Islamic supremacism, its expansionary ambitions, and the global scourge of jihad and barbaric practices that have entered Western countries. "Anti-islamophobia" motion M-103 and my firing for writing for Jihad Watch are wakeup calls.

I believe in human rights for all, the freedom of religion, free speech, equality for all, and protection of all innocents regardless of gender, class, creed and race, as any freedom-loving, democracy supporting individual and leader does and should.

# About the Author

CHRISTINE DOUGLASS-WILLIAMS is author of the book "The Challenge of Modernizing Islam," published by Encounter Books in New York City. She is Public Affairs and Media Consultant to the International Christian Embassy in Jerusalem Canada. Christine is also a former-federally appointed Director with the Canadian Race Relations Foundation and past advisor to the former Office of Religious Freedom in Canada.

Christine has conducted over 1,700 live television interviews as a current affairs talk show host and television producer on CTS TV in Burlington, capturing six international awards (including the Telly, Videographer and Omni Awards). A past political and crime news reporter and news room editor, Christine has also served as a regular national columnist with Metro News, where she also provided news analysis on political and diversity issues.

Her writings have appeared in many publications, including: the Middle East Quarterly, FrontPage Magazine, USA Today Online, Wall Street online and the Gatestone Institute in New York, where she has been on the Board of Governors. Christine is a regular writer for Jihad Watch, a project of the David Horowitz Freedom Center.

# REFERENCES


[1] "Canadian Race Relations Foundation Act (S.C. 1991, c. 8)," Justice Laws Website, Government of Canada, 1991.

[2] Robert Onley, "Keep Christine Williams on Canadian Race Relations Foundation Board & Protect Free Speech," Change.org.

[3] Robert Spencer, "Robert Spencer's Letter to Melanie Joly, Heritage Minister in the Trudeau Government—Is writing for Jihad Watch now a fireable offense?," Front Page Magazine, September 15, 2017.

[4] Daniel Pipes, "Please write letters of support for Christine Douglass-Williams, a potential victim of political correctness," Daniel Pipes, Middle East Forum, August 23, 2017.

[5] Michael Diamond, "On Trudeau, India, Islam in Canada and the risks associated with Radical Islam," Israpundit.org, Feb 23, 2018.

[6] Robert Spencer, "Canadian government appointee Christine Douglass-Williams under fire for writing for Jihad Watch," *Jihad Watch,* August 20, 2017.

[7] David Krayden, "Canada Inching Toward 'Islamophobia' Law," Daily Caller, January 26, 2017.

[8] Kathleen Harris, "5 things to know about the Commons motion on Islamophobia," CBC News, February 17, 2017.

[9] Christina Spencer, "Spencer: Islamophobia motion has been reduced to an exercise in cynicism," *Ottawa Citizen,* February 17, 2017.

[10] Christine Douglass-Williams, "Canadians Duped: A Victorious Day for Islamic Supremacists," *Jihad Watch,* March 25, 2017.

[11] Ibid.

[12] Ibid.

[13] Christine Douglass-Williams, "Canada: Quebec opposition parties reject making mosque shooting anniversary "day of action on Islamophobia," *Jihad Watch*, January 11, 2018.

[14] Christine Douglass-Williams, "Canadians Duped: A Victorious Day for Islamic Supremacists," *Jihad Watch*, March 25, 2017.

[15] Ibid.

[16] "NCCM Welcomes Unanimous Consent of Federal Motion Condemning Islamophobia," National Council of Canadian Muslims Press Release, October 2017.

[17] Alison Crawford, "Sharia and rules that govern religious practices in other faiths are not to be feared, spiritual leaders say," CBC News, September 20, 2017.

[18] Christine Douglass-Williams, "UK: Sharia courts operating beyond reach of British law and oppressing women," *Jihad Watch*, March 4, 2017.

[19] Jane Taber, "Muslim MPs express faith in Canadian tolerance amid anti-Islamic sentiment," *The Globe and Mail*, November 20, 2015.

[20] Christine Williams, "Christine Douglass-Williams fired from Canadian Race Relations Foundation for writing for Jihad Watch," *Jihad Watch,* December 21, 2017.

21 Daniel Greenfield, "Anti-Racist Activist Fired for speaking out against Muslim Brotherhood," *FrontPage Magazine*, December 22, 2017.

22 Tom Quiggin, "Islamic Supremacist Influence Behind the Firing of Christine Douglass-Williams From Federal Race Relations Agency?," *Jihad Watch*, December 26 2017.
Criminal Code (R.S.C., 1985, c. C-46), Justice Laws website, Government of Canada.

23 "Taking Action Against Systemic Racism and Religious Discrimination Including Islamophobia," Government Response to the 10th Report of the Standing Committee on Canadian Heritage, June 1, 2018.

24 Ibid.

25 Anthony Furey, "Some fears of Islam justified, human rights lawyer tells M103 committee," *Toronto Sun*, October 23, 2018.

26 "Taking Action Against Systemic Racism and Religious Discrimination Including Islamophobia," Government Response to the 10th Report of the Standing Committee on Canadian Heritage, June 1, 2018.

27 "MP Iqra Khalid Announces Liberal Government Response of $23 M Funding Initiatives in context of M103," Youtube, June 29, 2018.

28 Brian Daly, "RCMP probe into Islamist financing didn't end with IRFAN," *QMI Agency*, February 10, 2015.

29 Stewart Bell, "RCMP raids Muslim relief group's offices as Canada declares it a terrorist organization," *National Post*, April 29, 2014.

30 Brian Daly, "RCMP probe into Islamist financing didn't end with IRFAN," *QMI Agency*, February 10, 2015.

31 "Taking Action Against Systemic Racism and Religious Discrimination Including Islamophobia," Government Response to the 10th Report of the Standing Committee on Canadian Heritage, June 1, 2018.

32 Ibid.

33 "Taking Action Against Systemic Racism and Religious Discrimination Including Islamophobia," Government Response to the 10th Report of the Standing Committee on Canadian Heritage, June 1, 2018.

34 Ibid.

35 "Training and Workshops," National Council of Canadian Muslims website, https://www.nccm.ca/connect/training/

36 "Taking Action Against Systemic Racism and Religious Discrimination Including Islamophobia," Government Response to the 10th Report of the Standing Committee on Canadian Heritage, June 1, 2018.

37 "Justice Laws," Government of Canada, Justice Laws Website, http://laws-lois.justice.gc.ca/eng/acts/C-46/

38 "Taking Action Against Systemic Racism and Religious Discrimination Including Islamophobia," Government Response to the 10th Report of the Standing Committee on Canadian Heritage, June 1, 2018.

39 Mike Blanchfield, "Ex-religious freedom envoy claims summer job program shows 'totalitarian' tendency," The Canadian Press, May 9, 2018.

40 Candice Malcolm, "Another controversial Islamic group gets Summer Jobs Grant funding,," *Toronto Sun*, May 4, 2018.

41 "Yesterday in Parliament, House of Commons," CIJA, June 12, 2018. https://cija.ca/yip-june-12-2018/

42 Bradley Martin, "In Trudeau's Canada, Christians are Not Welcome," *Christian Post*, January 29, 2018.

43 "Conservative Party Of Canada – Minority Report Of The Standing Committee On Canadian Heritage On Systemic Racism And Religious Discrimination," House of Commons Canada, Accessed June 13, 2018.

44 Ibid.

45 "Cairo Declaration of Human Rights Adopted and Issued at the Nineteenth Islamic Conference of Foreign Ministers in Cairo, August 5, 1990," United Nations Human Rights Office of the High Commissioner, Accessed June 18, 2018.

46 "COMMISSION ON HUMAN RIGHTS REPORT ON THE FIFTY-FIFTH SESSION," 22 March - 30 April 1999. http://www.un.org/documents/ecosoc/docs/1999/e1999-23.pdf

47 "CHR 60 th session – Defamation of religions/Right to development --COMMISSION ADOPTS RESOLUTIONS ON COMBATING DEFAMATION OF RELIGIONS; RIGHT TO DEVELOPMENT," April 14, 2004. https://www.un.org/unispal/document/chr-60th-session-defamation-of-religions-right-to-development-press-release-excerpts/

48 "Defamation of Religions," The Legal Project – The Middle East Forum,  2018.

49 "Human Rights Council Sixteenth session Agenda item 9 Racism, racial discrimination, xenophobia and related form of intolerance, follow-up and implementation of the Durban Declaration and Programme of Action, A/HRC/RES/16/18," United Nations General Assembly 1 April 12,  2011.

50 Zadmin, "No such thing as Islamic terrorism, delegate tells UN confab on religious sensitivities," *UN Watch*, July 12, 2013.

51 Michael Curtis, "Islam and Free Speech: OIC vs. Universal Declaration of Human Rights," *Gatestone Institute*, February 8, 2012.

52 Shenaz Kermalli, "Justin Trudeau: Canada's agent for change?," *Aljazeera*, April 16, 2013.

53 "Omar Alghabra criticizes Canadian government's decision not to resort to Human Concern International to transfer relief money to Syria," Point de Bascule, March 28, 2013.

54 Judith Miller, "Some Charities Suspected of Terrorist Role," *New York Times*, February 19, 2000.

55 Brian Daly, "Canadian Muslim group funneled $300K to HAMAS-linked charity: Documents," Toronto Sun, January 28, 2015.

56 Ibid.

57 Ibid.

58 "Omar Alghabra led an organization that opposed the designation of HAMAS as a terrorist organization, he supported sharia law for Ontario and now he has been

appointed Parliamentary Secretary to the Minister of Foreign Affairs," Point de Bascule, December 16, 2015.

59 Stewart Bell, "Federal Court upholds government stopping funding to Canadian Arab Federation over concerns it appears to support terrorist organizations," *National Post*, January 7, 2014.

60 Ibid.

61 Ibid.

62 Ibid.

63 Nicolaas Van Rijn, "CanWest inserts word 'terrorist,' Groups asking for an inquiry," Canadian Arab Federation, September 18, 2004.

64 Ari Yashar, "Is Trudeau's new Foreign Minister Secretary a HAMAS backer?," Arutz Sheva, April 12, 2015.

65 Ibid.

66 Rick Kardonne, "Liberal candidate's position: 'I don't believe HAMAS wants elimination of Israel,' " Jewish tribune, January 5, 2006.

67 Ibid.

68 Ari Yashar, "Is Trudeau's new Foreign Minister Secretary a HAMAS backer?," Arutz Sheva, April 12, 2015.

69 38TH PARLIAMENT, 1ST SESSION SUBCOMMITTEE ON PUBLIC SAFETY AND NATIONAL SECURITY OF THE STANDING COMMITTEE ON JUSTICE, HUMAN RIGHTS, PUBLIC SAFETY AND EMERGENCY PREPAREDNESS, Tuesday, September 20, 2005.

70 Ari Yashar, "Is Trudeau's new Foreign Minister Secretary a HAMAS backer?," Arutz Sheva, April 12, 2015.

71 Michael Mostyn, "By Discouraging Criticism of Islam, M103 could make it harder to combat anti-Semitism," *National Post*, October 1, 2017.

72 Ibid.

73 John Rossomando, "IPT Exclusive: PR Firm Tied to CAIR Linked to Sliming of Maajid Nawaz," *The Investigative Project on Terrorism*, June 20, 2018.

74 Sarah Pruitt, "5 Things You May Not Know About Lincoln, Slavery And Emancipation," *History Stories*, September 21, 2012.

75 "What the Black Man Wants," Frederick Douglass April 1865 Speech at the Annual Meeting of the Massachusetts Anti-Slavery Society in Boston, Stephen Railton; Institute for Advanced Technology in the Humanities; Electronic Text Center, Charlottesville, Va., December 2005.

76 Blaine Winship, "Us-versus-them mentality and the Democratic Party," *The Hill*, July 27, 2016.

77 Ibid.

78 Ibid.

79 Chuck Ross, "FARRAKHAN: 'WE MUST RISE UP AND KILL THOSE WHO KILL US,'" *The Daily Caller*, August 4, 2015.

80 Ryan Lucas, "Extremist Leader Calls on Muslims Worldwide to Join Fight to Build Islamic State," *Toronto Star*, July 2, 2014.

81 William Kilpatrick, "Islam, Revolution, and Black Lives Matter," *Crisis Magazine*, July 14, 2016.

82 Wesley Lowery, "Aren't more white people than black people killed by police? Yes, but no.," *Washington Post*, July 11, 2016.

83 "How Much Are They Worth," L.A. Times, 2014-2016.

84 Olivia Beavers, Deirdre Walsh "House Democrats join protests over police shootings," *CNN*, July 8, 2018.

85 Ibid.

86 Ibid.

87 James Simpson, "Black Lives Matter: Racist Provocation with Radical Roots," *Capital Research Center*, September 21, 2016.

88 James Di Fiore, "Black Lives Matter Toronto Co-Founder Needs To Resign," *Huffington Post*, February 8, 2017.

89 "The Civil Rights Movement in America 1945-1968," The History Learning Site, 2018.

90 Lee Harris, "28-year-old Alexandria Ocasio-Cortez seeks 'generational change' after historic primary election victory," *ABC News*, June 27, 2018.

91 Allison Kaplan Sommer, "Alexandria Ocasio-Cortez Doubles Down on Slamming Israel's 'Occupation of Palestine'," *Haaretz*, July 16, 2018.

92 Judah Ari Gross, "HAMAS official: 50 of the 62 Gazans killed in border violence were our members," *The Times of Israel*, May 16, 2018.

93 John Nolte, "Media Fail—Trump's Approval Rating with Hispanics Jumps 10 Points," *Breitbart*, June 28, 2018

94 Abdur-Rahman Muhammad, "Whether or not Ground Zero mosque is built, U.S. Muslims have access to the American Dream," *New York Daily News*, September 5, 2010.

95 Ibid.

96 Jamie Ehrlich, "Maxine Waters encourages supporters to harass Trump administration officials," CNN, June 25, 2018.

97 Mordechai Sones, "US Professor: 'How come we don't have intifada in this country?'," *Israel National News*, July 27, 2017.

98 Ibid.

99 Bryan Preston, "Say, Remember that Time When Rahm Emanuel Had a Real Live Hate Group Patrol Chicago's Streets?," *PJ Media*, August 16, 2012.

100 Ben Schreckinger, "Has a Civil Rights Stalwart Lost Its Way?," *Politico*, July/August 2017.

101 David Huntley, "Counter-protest planned against Gays Against Sharia UK and Standing For Britain joint rally in Stockton," *Gazette Live UK*, July 23, 2018.

102 "Martin Luther King's I have a dream speech, August 28, 1963," American History From Revolution to Reconstruction and Beyond, GMW - University of Groningen, 1994-2012.

103 Niamh McIntyre, "Harvard University will hold first ever black only graduation ceremony," *UK Independent*, May 11, 2017.

104 Sarah Hoyt, "Separate and Unequal: Harvard Hosts Graduation for Black Students Only,"  P.J. Media, May 28, 2018.

105 Rowan Scarborough, "Obama's scrub of Muslim terms under question; common links in attacks," *The Washington Times*, Thursday, April 25, 2013.

106 Ibid.

107 "An Explanatory Memorandum: From the Archives of the Muslim Brotherhood in America," Center for Security Policy, May 25, 2013.

108 Rowan Scarborough, "Obama's scrub of Muslim terms under question; common links in attacks," *The Washington Times*, Thursday, April 25, 2013.

109 Christine Douglass-Williams, "Canada: Islamist-Leftist-Government Alliance Silences Free Speech," *Gatestone Institute*, January 8, 2018.

110 Robert Spencer, "JUSTIN TRUDEAU: CANADA'S OBAMA—The next Prime Minister of Canada will get along fine with the President," *FrontPage Magazine*, October 21, 2015.

111 Christine Douglass-Williams, "Shut Down Iran's Embassy in Canada," Gatestone Institute, August 9, 2012.

112 "Former Iranian Diplomat Explains Resignation," Radio Free Europe, March 15, 2010.

113 Christine Douglass-Williams, "Shut Down Iran's Embassy in Canada," Gatestone Institute, August 9, 2012.

114 Janice Kephart, "Court: Iran, Hezbollah partly responsible for 9/11," *The Washington Times,* December 30, 2011.

115 Mary Kay Linge, "Iranian official: We protected al-Qaeda terrorists before 9/11," *New York Post,* June 9,2018.

116 Ibid.

117 Michael Zennie, "Al Qaeda terror plot foiled after Canadian police arrest two over plan to blow up train to New York as it crossed Niagara Falls," *Daily Mail,* April 22, 2013.

118 Samantha Wright Allen, "With second trip to Tehran, feds inch closer to re-establishing diplomatic ties with Iran," *The Hill Times,* November 1, 2017.

119 Peter Zimonjic, "Iranian-Canadians, Liberal MP Call On Ottawa To Re-Establish Relations With Iran," CBC News, September 14, 2016.

120 Opposition Leader Andrew Scheer Twitter, June 13, 2018, https://twitter.com/andrewscheer/status/1006991938980077568?lang=en

121 Candice Malcolm, "Canadian jihadists are bolder than ever, meanwhile Trudeau weakens our laws," *Toronto Sun,* June 15, 2018

122 President Donald J. Trump, "National Security Strategy of the United States of America," December 2017.

123 Ibid.

124 Ibid.

125 Ibid.

126 Ibid.

127 David Ljunggren, Anna Mehler Paperny, "Justin Trudeau tweets messages of welcome to refugees as Trump travel ban sets in, *Global News*, January 28, 2017.

128 Sonja Puzic, "Record number of refugees admitted to Canada in 2016, highest since 1980," *CTV News*, April 24, 2017.

129 Janice Cheryl Beaver, "CRS Report for Congress U.S. International Borders: Brief Facts," Knowledge Services Group November 9, 2006.

130 Ben Lazarus, "'SHUT YOUR MOUTH' Corbyn ally shares message telling Rotherham sex abuse victims to be quiet 'for the good of diversity'," *The Sun*, August 22, 2018.

131 "Canadian Multiculturalism Act, R.S.C., 1985, c. 24 (4th Supp.)," Government Laws Website, accessed June 16, 2018, http://laws-lois.justice.gc.ca/eng/acts/C-18.7/page-1.html?wbdisable=true

132 Frank Gaffney Jr. and the Center for Security Policy," Extremism, Terrorism & Bigotry, American Defense League, 2017.

133 Stephen Johnson, "'Shutting people up raising awareness about Sharia law': Islam critic Ayaan Hirsi Ali hits back at Muslim women accusing her of being a 'white supremacist' – after she was forced to cancel Australian tour over security," *Daily Mail*, April 4, 2017

134 Itamar Marcus, Nan Jacques Zilberdik, "The Muslim Brotherhood - in its own words, PMW translation of Jihad is the Way by Mustafa Mashhur Leader of the Muslim Brotherhood in Egypt, from 1996 – 2002, *Palestinian Media Watch*, accessed July 14, 2018.

135 Ibid.

136 Marc A. Thiessen , "A horrifying look into the mind of 9/11's mastermind, in his own words," The *Washington Post*, November 28, 2016.

137 Mordechai Kedar and David Yerushalmi, "Shari'a and Violence in American Mosques," Middle East Quarterly Summer 2011 Volume 18: Number 3.

138 Christine Williams, *"The Challenge of Modernizing Islam"* (New York City: Encounter Books, 2017), 61, 68, 73.

139 Ibid., 83.

140 Scott Shane, *"*Saudis and Extremism: 'Both the Arsonists and the Firefighters', *" New York Times*, August 25, 2016.

141 Hollie McKay, "Critics say Turkish government using US mosques to play politics, spy on foes," *Fox News*, July 17, 2018.

142 Hjalmar Fridriksson, "Trúarleiðtogi múslima á Íslandi telur hryðjuverkin í London sviðsett að hluta," *DV.is*, June 7, 2017.

143 Brian Daly, "RCMP probe into Islamist financing didn't end with IRFAN," *QMI Agency*, February 10, 2015.

144 "CAIR-CAN condemns Point de Bascule "for slandering (Islamist) conference participants and guests,"" Pointdebasculecanada, December 12, 2012.

145 Matt Drake, "Toronto police name 'horrific' GUNMAN who killed two and injured 12 as Faisal Hussain," *Express*, July 24, 2018.

146 Anthony Furey, "Meet the spin doctor behind the Hussain family statement," *Toronto Sun*, July 25, 2018.

147 Ibid.

148 Bernie Farber, Mira Sucharov, "We must overcome Islamophobia in 2018," *The Star*, January 2, 2018.

149 Rachel Ehrenfeld, "Toronto's mass shooting "tragedy" (Justin Trudeau), "wasn't hatred" (Bernie Farber)," *American Center for Democracy*, June 24, 2018.

150 "THE PERCEPTION & REALITY OF "IMPORTED CONFLICT" IN CANADA (KEY FINDINGS SUMMARY)," The Mosaic Institute, March 2014.

151 "Canada in a Trump World," The Mosaic Institute, February 28, 2017.   The Mosaic Institute has a longtime relationship with the NCCM and endorsed its "Charter for Inclusive Communities."

152 "Charter for Inclusive Communities, NCCM Website, June 2016.

153 Tamara Lush, Rob Gillies, "Toronto shooter's neighbors unaware of his mental illness," *Associated Press*, June 25, 2018.

154 Joe Warmington, "Danforth shooter was 'armed for war,' sources say," *Toronto Sun*, June 25, 2018.

155 Ibid.

156 Joe Warmington, "Was Danforth attack terror, or terrorism?," *Toronto Sun*, July 25, 2018.

157 Jennifer Yang, "Board member of anti-racism agency fired amid accusations of Islamophobic commentary," *Toronto Star*, December 21, 2017.

158 Ibid.

159 Ibid.

160 Ibid.

161 Ben Cohen,  "US Ambassador Haley Rips Arab, Islamic States for Posturing at UN on Palestinian Question,," *Algemeiner*, July 24.

www.ingramcontent.com/pod-product-compliance
Lightning Source LLC
Chambersburg PA
CBHW061722250726
48657CB00002B/728